D0871977

AN INTRODUCTION TO THE
PHILOSOPHY OF NATURE

AN INTRODUCTION TO THE
PHILOSOPHY OF NATURE

BY

Henry J. Koren, C.S.Sp., S.T.D.

Third Impression

1962
Duquesne University Press
Pittsburgh, Pa.

BY THE SAME AUTHOR

An Introduction to the Science of Metaphysics. XIX
and 291 pages. Published by The Herder Book Company, St. Louis. $4.00. Third impression, 1960.

An Introduction to the Philosophy of Animate Nature.
XIII and 341 pages. Published by The Herder Book
Company, St. Louis. $4.00. Fourth impression, 1961.

Readings in the Philosophy of Nature. XI and 401 pages.
Published by The Newman Press, Westminster. $2.25.
Second impression, 1960.

PREFACE

The purpose of this book is rather modest. It does not aim at new theories, but simply intends to present a suitable text for undergraduate courses in the philosophy of nature.[1] The regrettable scarcity of such texts, coupled with the fact that practically all of them are either out of date or not sufficiently adapted to the undergraduate student, induced the author to undertake this work.

Undoubtedly, the book is not without imperfections. The task of writing a perfect text in this subject matter requires almost superhuman powers. The reasons are that the undergraduate program usually allots only three semester hours for the philosophy of nature and that the students taking this course often have only a very elementary acquaintance with physical science. Thus the author was forced to compress intricate philosophical problems, explain physical theories in a language that can be understood by the non-science major, and confront these theories with the findings of philosophy. If sometimes he may seem to "run in where angels fear to tread," the critical reader is requested to consider the limitations under which this book had to be written.

The text presupposes that the student has followed a course in general metaphysics. One who has no metaphysical notions of being, analogy, substance, causality, etc. will find it almost impossible to follow a course in the philosophy of nature, unless, of course, the necessary

---

[1]The philosophy of *animate* nature considers living bodies precisely as living bodies. The philosophy of nature attains these living bodies insofar as they have certain characteristics in common with non-living beings. For this reason we have abstained from calling this book a philosophy of *inanimate* nature.

metaphysical introduction is supplied by the teacher prior to the subject matter in which the metaphysical notions play a role.

The mention of general metaphysics as a prerequisite for the philosophy of nature could conceivably cause some critics to start at once crying "Wolff." It may, therefore, not be superfluous to point out that one can speak of general and special metaphysics without attributing to these terms the same sense as Christian von Wolff. "Special" metaphysics does not necessarily mean that we take the major premise from metaphysics and the minor from science. It may also indicate that we are concerned with the philosophical study of being insofar as being manifests itself in a limited realm of reality. This is the sense in which the term is used here.

Where historical developments are not incorporated into the text, only the briefest mention could be made of divergent views in *Historical Notes*. Usually the reasons supporting these views are not mentioned nor is any critical analysis made of them. To do justice to them would have required extensive discussions of their general philosophical setting and thus exceeded the limited scope of this book. The brief mention made of the various views is sufficient, however, to have the interested student search for monographs about the philosopher in question or consult a detailed history of philosophy.

The *Suggested Readings* at the end of each chapter contain many entries which develop the subject matter more broadly. As usual, references are made also to the writings of Aristotle and to those of Thomas Aquinas, but it may not be amiss to warn the student that precisely in the philosophy of nature these ancient works intermingle many antiquated physical theories with philosophical considerations. Great caution, therefore, is necessary in reading them, for such physical theories are extraneous to the philosophy of nature.

Preface

Many suggested titles refer to works of which extracts are contained in the author's READINGS IN THE PHILOSOPHY OF NATURE (Newman Press, 1958). This collection of readings contains a fairly large selection of texts exemplifying various trends and currents of thought and thus constitutes a supplement to this book.

Summaries have been added at the end of each chapter so that the student can more easily find the main line of thought developed in the chapter. Review Questions at the end of the book facilitate the work of preparing for examinations. Paragraphs marked with an asterisk contain material which, at the discretion of the lecturer, may be omitted without serious loss in continuity of thought.

The preparation of this text derived a good deal of inspiration from the stimulating lectures given at Duquesne University by its Visiting Professors, such as Dr. Andrew G. van Melsen, Dr. P. Henry van Laer, and Dr. Herman Leo Van Breda. In addition, I have made frequent use of their publications, as well as those of Professor Peter Hoenen. While I do not wish these gentlemen to be held responsible for the contents of this book, I cannot abstain from acknowledging here my dependence on them. My thanks are due also to Dr. Andrew G. van Melsen, Dr. John P. Rowan, and the Rev. Norman F. Lord, C.S.Sp., for reading the work in typescript and volunteering their valuable criticism.

Duquesne University,
Pittsburgh, Pa. October 29, 1959.

HENRY J. KOREN, C.S.Sp.

TABLE OF CONTENTS

Table of Contents

Table of Contents

Table of Contents

CHAPTER ONE

INTRODUCTION

1. PRELIMINARY REMARKS

1. The philosophical study which we are about to begin endeavors to investigate the character of the inanimate material world on the level of being. By saying "inanimate" we indicate that our considerations here will be restricted to the material world generally, abstracting from the fact that some beings are alive.[1] By material world we mean not only the things in our familiar everyday surroundings, but also the celestial bodies reached by the astronomer's telescope as well as the subatomic world of nuclear science. It extends to whatever is material and all its determinations.

2. The question what this material world or any of its parts really is allows various correct answers. It depends on the intention we have in mind when we ask the question whether the answer will be considered satisfactory or not. An example may make this clear. Let us suppose that I want to know what water is. According to the intention prompting me to ask this question, I may address myself to a chemist, a physicist, a philosopher, a housewife, etc. The chemist will reply: water is a compound of two parts of hydrogen and one part of oxygen; the physicist will say that it is a colorless liquid with a specific gravity of one, which boils at 212°F. at sea level, freezes at 32°F., etc.; and the housewife will answer that it is the liquid you get from the faucet. While each of these answers is correct as far as it goes, none exhaustively replies to the question what water is. All of them consider water merely

---

[1]For a study of the world of living bodies, see the author's *Introduction to the Philosophy of Animate Nature*, Herder, 1955. Hereafter quoted as *Animate Nature*.

from a particular point of view. Therefore, they are only partial answers. The same will be true of the philosophical answer to the question. Whatever the philosophical reply may be, it remains a purely partial and incomplete answer that will be satisfactory only from the philosophical point of view. To obtain a complete and exhaustive reply to the question, I would have to study water from every possible viewpoint.

What has been said here of water applies to the whole material world. Many identical questions may be asked about it and receive different correct but partial replies. Accordingly, we should never lose sight of the fact that a philosophical study of matter cannot aspire at supplying all answers to questions regarding the nature of the material world. It has its own restricted viewpoint or formal object, as it is technically called, and cannot even attempt to go beyond this viewpoint without denying its very nature. The same is true of any other science studying matter. Hence the only problems we are interested in here are philosophical ones regarding the nature of matter and its primary determinations.

2. STARTING POINT AND METHOD OF THE PHILOSOPHY OF NATURE

3. What exactly is meant when we say that we want to investigate the nature of matter *philosophically?* The reply to this question necessitates an inquiry into the starting point and method of the philosophy of nature and their distinction from the starting points and methods of other sciences of matter.

Empirical Verifiability. As was pointed out in general metaphysics,[2] our intellectual knowledge takes its beginning in sense experience. The data received from the

---

[2]Cf. the author's *Introduction to the Science of Metaphysics.* Herder, 1955 (hereafter quoted as *Metaphysics*), No. 2. For a detailed study see his *Animate Nature,* Ch. 13.

senses supply the intellect with the necessary material for its own operations. The intellect judges and interprets these sense data. The way man's intellect proceeds in selecting certain data and using them to arrive at insights into the material world may be called scientific method in the broad sense of the term. Two fundamentally very different methods are available. One of these consists in selecting data and theorizing about them in such a way that a return to sense experience can be made to verify the conclusions. Such a method is typical of the so-called experimental sciences. If, for instance, someone asserts that water boils at 200° F. at sea level, the truth or falsity of this statement can be readily checked by performing an experiment. Of course, not every physical or chemical statement is as easily verified as this example. Nevertheless, it remains true that at least in principle any assertion which properly belongs to the experimental sciences can be verified by an intellectual return to sense experience. Evidently, the availability of such an experimental verification constitutes one of the great attractions and strong points of these sciences.

On the other hand, we should not exaggerate the value of this verifiability. If it sometimes induces people to claim that statements regarding nature which cannot be verified experimentally may not be be called true, certain, or even meaningful, enthusiasm for experimentalism has led to dangerously misjudging the capacity of the intellect and narrowing the realms of knowledge open to human inquiry. We should keep in mind that verification through sense experience requires that our conclusion retain an element which is subject to sense observation, for otherwise the intellect's return to the senses could not verify such a conclusion. But what right does anyone have *a priori* to shackle the intellect in its search for truth and limit it to judgments that retain sense perceptible elements? Of course, one may legitimately insist that the intellect's conclusions be always subject to some form of verification, but how could anyone justify that arbitrary restriction of verification to sense experience? The very attempt to impose this limitation constitutes an internal contradiction, for it itself cannot be verified by sense experience.

4. *Non-Empirical Verification.* Accordingly, we cannot *a priori* reject the possibility of an intellectual approach to the material world which conceivably could reach conclusions that are beyond verification by the senses. The realm of this approach is reached as soon as a statement about the material world is made which does not retain in its predicate any characteristic that is either directly or indirectly perceptible by the senses. Verification is still possible here, but in a way that differs considerably from the method used in experimental science. It will have to consist in 1) a careful search to see whether the experiential starting point is true and not subject to reasonable doubt; 2) strict observance of the laws of reasoning. For, if the starting point is true and the reasoning process correct, it follows of necessity that the conclusion must be true. Philosophy, and in particular the philosophy of nature, claims to be such an intellectual approach to the material world.

a. The Experiential Starting Point

From these considerations we can readily see that any effort to arrive at philosophical insights into nature has to begin by diligently establishing the experiential data which give rise to its problems.

5. *Scientific or Pre-Scientific Experience?* A priori speaking, there is no reason to claim that these data must be sought exclusively either in the results attained by experimental science or in pre-scientific experience. As a matter of fact, however—and this point will become clear in the course of this study—the enormously rich data

Introduction

accumulated by science in the last two or three centuries
offer but little that can serve to enrich the philosophy of
nature by leading it to *new* philosophical insights. The
reason for this situation is not far to seek. What philosophy
wonders about are mostly problems so primordial that the
necessary experiential starting point is readily discovered
without an appeal to the results of scientific experiments.
For instance, it endeavors to understand how it is possible
for many bodies to possess the same nature. This problem
arises from the observation that many bodies act and are
acted upon in the same way and thereby indicate that they
have the same nature. Evidently, no complex scientific
experiments are required to establish the correctness of
the observational starting point. To give another example,
when philosophy tries to understand how it is possible for
an individual to act intermittently, it finds its starting
point in the experiential evidence that at least some types
of activity occur intermittently.

Another reason for the uselessness of the results obtained
by modern experimental science for *new* philosophical
insights lies in the fundamentally different attitude of
both studies of the material world. The two do not move
on the same level, so that their paths do not cross. As a
result, one can do very little to enlighten the other in
its proper sphere.

6. *Negative Importance of Science for Philosophy.*
While it is true that experimental science can offer but
little positive aid in the philosophical study of nature by
leading it to new insights, it plays a very important role
in a *negative* way. The same is true of philosophy with
respect to science. Theoretically it is easy enough to
separate philosophy and experimental science by pointing
to their differences in viewpoint and method, but in practice
difficulties arise because of the human beings who devote
themselves to science or philosophy. They do not always

5

realize exactly where the boundaries lie between the two realms of knowledge. Thus it can easily happen that the philosopher unwittingly tries to solve by means of his own method problems which belong to the domain of experimental science. Reversely, the scientist may do the same and innocently endeavor to answer questions that exceed his professional competence.

We advisedly say "unwittingly" and "innocently," for there can be no question of denying any human being the right to pursue philosophy or science or even both if he so desires. The danger lies not so much in the philosophical studies of a scientist or in the scientific work of a philosopher as in the failure to realize that one passes from philosophy to science or vice versa. The history of the seventeenth and eighteenth centuries provides abundant examples of philosophers of nature who did not suspect that they were spending most of their time in vainly trying to solve scientific questions by means of the philosophical method.

There are also many instances in which scientists unwittingly let philosophical views influence their theories. When, e.g., the nineteenth century scientist thought that the results of his research forced him to reject free will, he did not realize that he had added the philosophy of universal mechanism to his scientific studies. Sometimes even the very terminology used in experimental science has connotations deriving from tacitly assumed philosophical views This is exemplified by such expressions as the "creation" and "annihilation" of matter, the transformation of "matter" into energy, and the "free choice" of moment of disintegration.

The reason for this state of affairs appears to be that man is never satisfied with the partial knowledge supplied by either philosophy or science and therefore attempts to remedy the deficiency by adding complementary considerations drawn from a different viewpoint. Lacking, as is so often the case, the necessary training in the procedures proper to this new mode of looking at the object of his interest, it is not surprising if he makes unwarranted assertions and shows a woeful absence of even the most elementary insights into the nature of either science or philosophy. For this reason scientists and philosophers can aid each other by sounding a due warning when either party unwittingly oversteps the boundaries of his chosen field of studies.

Although the work done in this direction was called above the negative aid of scientists to philosophers and vice versa, the use of this term does not mean that this work is not very important. If it were not for this constant corrective labor, many would unwittingly overstep the limits of their competence. Of course not every philosopher is capable of pointing out the transgressions of the scientist, nor is every scientist in a position to show philosophers where they have gone beyond their chosen field. In general, only a specialist who is equally at home in both science and philosophy has the necessary qualifications for pioneering labor in this area.

7. *Positive Aid of Science to Philosophy.* Above, it was pointed out that experimental science can contribute "but *little* positive aid" to the philosophy of nature. We must now indicate in what this *little* consists. In the first place, the results of science may supply new examples to illustrate philosophical principles. One has only to consult almost any page in an ancient Greek or medieval treatise of the philosophy of nature to see how often the philosophers of those times took their illustrations from contemporaneous, now antiquated, science. Even if the philosophical insights of those times are considered to retain their value, it is obvious that the examples used have to be replaced by others which are in accord with the modern developments of experimental science. At least, they should be chosen in such a way that they are not open to scientific objections.

Secondly, modern science can make a positive contribution insofar as its studies may open new areas in which already acquired philosophical insight can find an application. The discovery, for example, that the sun, planets, and stars are composed of the same kind of matter as the earth makes it possible for philosophy to dispense with the modifications of hylomorphism which an earlier age had thought necessary because of faulty ideas about the physical nature of celestial bodies. Likewise, the progress of science forces the philosopher to proceed with considerable circumspection when he attempts to apply his concepts of individuality and substantiality to material objects. He can no longer consider any "natural" body as an individual substance and any "artificial" body as an aggregate, but has to recall the analogous nature of his concepts before he may attempt to determine individual substantiality in a concrete way.

Thirdly, it is not *a priori* excluded that data discovered by science may lead to entirely new insights. However, the probability that such data will be discovered does not seem to be very great. Science would have to discover a fundamental aspect of all matter which does not reveal itself at all in pre-scientific experience. As a matter of fact, the contributions hitherto made by science to the philosophy of nature are reducible to the categories enumerated in the preceding paragraphs.[3]

8. *Pre-Scientific Starting Point.* Thus far our considerations have led us to the assertion that the data of experimental science are almost wholly irrelevant to the acquisition of new insights into the philosophy of nature. Does this mean therefore that the philosophical study of matter must be based primarily on pre-scientific experi-

---

[3]It is to be noted that we are speaking here about the philosophy of nature in the strict sense of the term and not about the philosophy of physical science. Evidently, the philosophical reflection on the methods of science is much more intimately connected with science than is the philosophy of nature.

ence? While the answer will be in the affirmative, it must be made clear at once that pre-scientific experience is not to be identified with inaccurate knowledge. Of course, it is true that in many cases pre-scientific knowledge is false because it is nothing but a more or less primitive interpretation of appearances. The geocentric view of the universe and the Aristotelian theory of four elements may be quoted as examples of such a primitive type of pre-scientific knowledge.

In general, we may consider as primitive any kind of knowledge of nature that is subject to being corrected by subsequent experimental research. However, apart from such primitive knowledge there are also other pre-scientific aspects in experiential data with respect to which we do not have to fear that subsequent experimental research will force us to modify our view. This will be the case at least when this pre-scientific knowledge is embedded in the very method of science in such a way that science itself takes the truth of this knowledge for granted. In other words, the entire value of experimental science itself stands or falls with the acceptance or rejection of these aspects of pre-scientific experience.

Let us give a few examples of such pre-scientific knowledge. Although science may progressively arrive at new insights into the nature of the various changes that occur in matter, it never questions the fact that changes do occur. The absolute denial of change would take away the value of scientific explanations which are concerned with the way particular changes take place. If no changes ever occur, we will have to reject as meaningless the physical and chemical laws that are proposed as explanations or descriptions of the interaction of material things.

Another example is that different material objects react in the same way and therefore can be classified as beings endowed with the same properties and nature. For instance, the periodic system does not merely list the individual samples of iron, copper, etc. used by scientists in drawing up the system, but is supposed to apply to all iron, all copper, etc. It is simply taken for granted or presupposed that the same kind of nature can be multiplied "to infinity" in individuals. The denial of this multiplication would strip the statements of science of their general value for entire classes. Without the multiplication, all a scientist could do would be to engage in never ending descriptions of individual actions of individual things, without ever being able to arrive at an insight into a pattern of action or even at a classification.

Accordingly, by choosing this pre-scientific or primary type of experience as the starting point of the philosophy of nature, we eliminate the fear that the development of science would force us to abandon our conclusions because of the primitive character of our starting point.

b. Method of the Philosophy of Nature

9. *Induction.* The method of the philosophy of nature is inductive in gathering the necessary data which constitute the experiential starting point. However, as has been pointed out above, most of these data are so readily available in experience that usually a simple statement of the starting point is sufficient and there is no need to conduct a formal process of induction.

10. *Analysis.* Once the experiential starting point is established, the intellect will analyze it for its philosophical content, i.e., it will examine the data of experience to see what problems they raise on the level of being and its intelligibility. To clarify this statement somewhat, let us recall that one of the most fundamental philosophical insights and convictions of man is the intelligibility of being.[4]

Whatever is can be understood; being is intelligible. Therefore, the material world is intelligible in all its aspects

---

[4] Cf. the author's *Metaphysics,* nos. 81 ff., 114 ff.

and not merely with respect to the inter-relationships existing between the various bodily beings of this world. Accordingly, the philosophy of nature endeavors to understand how the most fundamental characteristics of matter—those contained in the primary experience of matter—can be reconciled with being. To say it differently, if, for instance, change exists (occurs) in bodies, or if there exists a multiplicity of individuals possessing the same specific material nature, then it must be possible to express in terms of being what this means, it must be possible to say what kind of a *being* such a material thing is.

11. *Reflection.* The analysis of the experiential data is followed by a reflection which considers the whole matter in the light of metaphysical insights. The intellect examines material things in the light of principles that apply to all beings or at least to all finite beings. In this reflection we must take care not to lose sight of the analogous nature of these general metaphysical principles. Their quasi-mechanical application to the realm of nature would be almost meaningless, for, as was pointed out in the study of metaphysics,[5] such analogous principles are absolutely different and only relatively the same with respect to different beings. Therefore, their content has to be rendered more precise with respect to the material world.

12. *Deduction.* In the course of this reflection the intellect arrives deductively at certain insights into the nature of the material world. Subsequently, it may use these insights to proceed deductively to further conclusions. In this way it is possible to construct an interconnected whole of conclusions that allow us a measure of philosophical understanding of material being.

Let us add immediately that the insight thus obtained is not very rich. Compared with the huge wealth of under-

---

[5]Cf. *op. cit.*, nos. 36 ff., 127.

standing of nature which the experimental sciences have gathered together, the philosophy of nature appears poor and, at first sight, even unimportant. However, here we should not forget that the few insights it manages to gain from experience are concerned to a large extent with questions on which ultimately depends the whole value of the structures created by experimental science, at least if we are to consider these sciences as knowledge of the real. Thus the importance of the philosophy of nature should not be judged by the richness and variety of its conclusions, but by the fundamental role it plays in man's efforts to arrive at a more integral knowledge of the world around him.

3. DIFFERENT OPINIONS ABOUT THE PHILOSOPHY OF NATURE

13. Perhaps no other philosophical treatise is the subject of more widely divergent views regarding its character than is the philosophy of nature. Historically speaking, this situation arose mainly from the conflict between experimental scientists and philosophers which became very bitter in the seventeenth century and continues to exist even in our days.

Prior to the seventeenth century there was hardly any question of an autonomous science of the material world. The few data and theories which we would now classify as belonging to experimental science were simply incorporated into philosophy and constituted together with the study of matter on the level of being so-called "physics" or the philosophy of nature. With few exceptions, notably St. Thomas,[6] hardly anyone appears to have been aware

---

[6]*In Boethium de Trinitate*, q.VI, a.2 (English translation Armand Maurer, *The Division and Methods of the Sciences*, Toronto, 1953, pp. 62 f.). Cf. Andrew G. van Melsen, *The Philosophy of Nature*, 3rd ed., Pittsburgh, 1961, pp. 90 ff., and P. Henry van Laer, *The Philosophy of Science*, Part One, Pittsburgh, 1956, pp. 26 ff.

of the fact that there existed a possiblity of developing two different approaches to the world of matter—one that would return to sense experience for its verification, and the other strictly philosophical. The nascent experimental sciences themselves were presented as new *philosophies*[7] destined to replace the system hitherto in vogue. Only very gradually did it dawn upon scientists and philosophers alike that they were engaged in studying matter from different viewpoints which did not contradict each other. Subsequently, the philosophy of nature slowly began to rid itself of the heavy crust of antiquated considerations, foreign to its nature and methods, which had accumulated about it in the course of the preceding centuries. It retains now only problems which, in the words of Thomas Aquinas, are concerned "with potency, with act, with unity or anything of the sort" and therefore can be called "a part of metaphysics because they are considered in the same manner as is the being which is the subject of metaphysics."[8]

Scientists on the other hand, blinded as they were by the success of their methods, refused for a long time to admit any other approach to nature than their own and therefore rejected the validity of a philosophical study of matter. Although it is true that nowadays the attitude of many scientists is far more modest and admits the limitations of their methods, the outspoken rejection of the philosophy of nature is not yet entirely a thing of the past.

We, therefore, record here briefly the most important views of both philosophers and scientists about the character and value of the philosophy of nature. Lack of space,

---

[7]Cf., for instance, the title of Newton's work *Mathematical Principles of Natural Philosophy* and that of Dalton's study *A New System of Chemical Philosophy*. Another relic of the past pointing to the same confusion is that even nowadays the successful graduate student in the experimental sciences is granted a doctorate in *philosophy*.

[8]*In Boethium de Trinitate,* q.V, a.1, ad 6 (English translation, p. 15).

however, prevents us from making a critical examination of all these views, especially because many of them would have to be considered within the framework of the general philosophical standpoint of which they are an expression.

14. *The Preparatory Stage of Experimental Science.* According to Richard von Mises,[9] only experimental science can provide valid explanations for the data of experience. However, at its inception a new science is always philosophical. Man desires to expand the boundaries of his knowledge and therefore progresses beyond the limits of scientific verification. Gradually, however, the advance of science engulfs the areas of primitive philosophical speculations and incorporates its valuable elements into its systems of verified truths. Thus the role of philosophy is limited to preparing the stage for experimental science.

15. *Petrified Science.* Philipp Frank[10] claims that the philosophy of nature amounts to little else than the stubborn refusal of non-scientists to abandon antiquated physical theories. By means of an historical analysis of the past three centuries, he attempts to support this point. Although it is true that to a large extent the philosophers of nature in the past lent themselves to such an interpretation, it should not be forgotten that this past historical situation of philosophy does not allow us to draw a conclusion about its true character because of the then reigning confusion of science and philosophy.

16. *Synthesis of the Results of Science.* A large number of scientists, such as Einstein, Heisenberg, Bohr, and de Broglie, see no room for a philosophy of nature except as a speculative prolongation of modern research that remains on the same level as the physical sciences themselves. For them, to philosophize about nature means to search for

---

[9]*Kleines Lehrbuch des Positivismus,* The Hague, 1939, pp. 300 ff.
[10]*Modern Science and its Philosophy,* Cambridge, 1949, pp. 207 ff.

an ever more inclusive synthesis of the results attained by the different branches of scientific research. For this reason "the theoretical scientists who have shown such a remarkable ability in their coordination of natural facts are the men best fitted to construct a philosophy of nature."[11] Obviously, in this view, the philosophical study of matter would be nothing but a treatise of physical theory. So far as the traditional notion of philosophy is concerned, such a study would be philosophical only in name but not in content.

17. *Logical Analysis of Scientific Propositions.* Moritz Schlick and others see room for a philosophy of nature within the general framework of their logical positivism.[12] Its task, they say, is "to interpret the meaning of the propositions of natural science," i.e. all sentences purporting to express the real, in order to see whether or not they are logically meaningful.

18. *Philosophical Analysis of Scientific Methods.* Henry Margenau,[13] Arthur Eddington[14] and others admit the possibility of a philosophy of nature insofar as the methods of science are subjected to a philosophical analysis. But they take the term "philosophical" in the Kantian or neo-Kantian sense as the investigation of the thought forms used in science and interpret them either in the classical Kantian sense of *a priori* laws of thinking or at least as forms that *de facto* do occur in science.

19. *Philosophical Reflection on the Results of Science.* Many others, such as Bavink, Mitterer, and Seiler,[15] consider it legitimate to philosophize about nature, but they claim that this reflection should take its starting point in

---

[11]A. d'Abro, *The Evolution of Scientific Thought,* New York, 1950, p. 355.
[12]*Philosophy of Nature,* New York, 1949, pp. 1 ff.
[13]*The Nature of Physical Reality,* New York, 1950, pp. 12 ff.
[14]*The Philosophy of Physical Science,* Cambridge, 1949, pp. 16 ff.
[15]*Philosophie der unbelebten Natur,* Olten, 1948, pp. 78 ff.

the data of science for, so they say, scientific research has opened up entirely new hitherto unsuspected philosophical vistas and allow us to give our thinking a secure foundation. Any other kind of philosophical study about nature deserves the scornful epithet, so often applied to it by men of science, of being a collection of antiquated views.

20. *Philosophical Approach to Nature.* Finally there is a large group of thinkers who claim that there is room for an autonomous philosophy of nature which has its own approach to the world of matter and does not depend on experimental science. Proponents of this trend differ widely among themselves as to what this philosophical approach should be.

Nineteenth century German idealism, represented by Hegel, conceived nature as one of the three dialectical phases in the self-development of the absolute concept, a phase in which the idea finds itself in a fallen state, unable to control its own manifestations and therefore marked by contradictions and impotence to remain true to its own categories. The total divorce of philosophy from experience, which characterized this view, caused such a violent reaction against the philosophical study of nature that for many years the mere mention of the name was enough to expose one to scorn. Thus it is not surprizing that this type of philosophical approach has almost totally disappeared from the scene.

Nicolai Hartmann, Eduard May and others advocate a *phenomenological* philosophy of nature. According to Hartmann,[16] the time has not yet come to construct a definite philosophical system. For the time being, all philosophy can do is to search for the problems which lie at the basis of all philosophical systems, treat them

---

[16]*Philosophie der Natur, Berlin,* 1950, pp. 14 ff. It should be noted that there is more than one way in which phenomenology can be used in philosophy. However, this point lies beyond the scope of the present study.

phenomenologically and thus lay bare the most fundamental categories of being. Where these categories are concerned with the lowest strata of being—the physical material and the organic—we have to do with the philosophy of nature.

A third group, to which belong most of the modern philosophers who remain within the *Aristotelian-Thomistic* tradition, admits a philosophy of nature that is based upon experience but proceeds to conclusions of a genuinely philosophical nature. They do not reject the data of science, but insist that these data cannot be simply transposed into philosophy to prove or disprove any truly philosophical position. As representatives of this group we may name Maritain, Renoirte, van Melsen, Hoenen, and Luyten.[17] As we will see presently, there are still considerable differences among the proponents of this view.

4. PHILOSOPHY OF NATURE AND THE CRITIQUE OF THE SCIENCES

21. Alongside the philosophy of nature in the strict sense of the term, there is room for a critique of the experimental study of nature.[18] Its object is to investigate the character of man's *knowledge* of nature. As such, it is a kind of epistemology which is concerned with the evaluation of the methods proper to these sciences and of the physical explanations given to the data of experience. This critique may be called philosophy in a broader sense of the term and, more specifically, the philosophy of the science of nature. As we have seen in the preceding section, this type of study is often considered to be the only legitimate philosophical approach to nature.

---

[17]"De actueele stelling der traditioneele natuurphilosophie," *Tijdschrift voor Philosophie,* vol. 8 (1949), pp. 210 ff.

[18]Cf. Herman L. Van Breda "Natuurphilosophie, positieve natuurwetenschappen en critiek der natuurwetenschappen," *Streven,* 1944, pp. 215 ff.

The critique of the natural sciences does not constitute the primary object of the present book. However, frequently we will refer to it—namely, whenever the claim is made that this critique has consequences for our philosophical knowledge of nature itself.

5. THE DIVISION OF THE SCIENCES AND THE PHILOSOPHY OF NATURE

22. According to a famous theory of Thomas Aquinas,[19] in scientific knowledge our intellect lays hold of reality in three distinct ways by viewing the object of its consideration under different aspects. These three ways are often called the three degrees of abstraction. In the first degree the intellect leaves behind (abstracts *from*) individual characteristics, but retains (abstracts) all common sense-perceptible features; in the second, it abstracts from all sense-perceptible characteristics and retains only the "imaginable" element of quantity; in the third, it leaves behind everything that is either sensible or imaginable and considers its object on the level of being. On the basis of this theory, he classified the sciences of his time into three groups—viz., physics or philosophy of nature (first degree), mathematics (second degree), and metaphysics (third degree).

In addition to this division according to abstraction, St. Thomas[20] pointed out corresponding levels on which these sciences terminate, i.e., the levels of knowability proper to their object. On the first level, the object is known in a way which allows a return to the senses, and therefore verification by sense experience is typical of the

---

[19]Cf. Thomas Aquinas, *In Boethium de Trinitate,* qq. V and VI. English text, *The Division and Methods of the Sciences,* by Armand Maurer, *C. S. B.,* Toronto, 1953.

[20]*Ibid.,* q. VI, aa.1 and 2; English translation, pp. 46 ff. Cf. P. Henry van Laer, *The Philosophy of Science, Part One,* Pittsburgh, 1956, pp. 26 ff.

physical sciences which work on this level. On the second level, the object is studied in the way it exists only in our imagination—namely, as devoid of all characteristics except quantity; therefore, it is to the imagination that the intellect must return for the verification of our statements. This manner of verification is typical of mathematics.[21] On the third level, the object is considered in such a way that verification is possible only in the intellect because here we are concerned with something than can neither be sensed nor imagined, but only understood. It is here that St. Thomas placed metaphysics.

The question is whether this medieval view still retains its value as a basis for the division of the sciences, especially because nowadays there are so many branches of learning that existed not at all or only in a very embryonic state in the Middle Ages. Various replies are given to this question. Some, such as Joseph T. Clark,[22] reject it as wholly antiquated, others maintain its validity, but differ in their explanation. Three views present themselves for consideration.

23. *Philosophy of Nature and Physical Science are Specifically the Same.* William H. Kane[23] and other members of the River Forest Group claim that physical science and philosophy of nature constitute one science, which they place on the first level of knowledge. A difficulty against this view is the following strange phenomenon. A metaphysician, who supposedly is concerned with a totally different kind of science (on the third level), has

---

[21]The statement remains applicable to modern mathematical systems if it is taken to mean that their conclusions are verified by a return to the fundamental axioms which we imagine to be "true," e.g., the axiom that through a point outside a line no parallel line can be drawn.

[22]*Proceedings of the American Catholic Philosophical Association,* 1953, pp. 55 f.

[23]"The Nature and Extent of the Philosophy of Nature," *The Thomist,* 1944, pp. 222 ff.

no difficulty whatsoever in following a discussion of, say, the matter-form theory proposed in the philosophy of nature, because the language, methods, principles and mode of verification are all familiar to him. On the other hand, an expert in theoretical physics who does not have any training in philosophy would be at a loss to say what the discussion is all about, just as vice versa a philosopher without scientific background would feel like a fish out of water if he were suddenly transferred into a convention of theoretical physicists. It would be difficult to explain this situation on the assumption that the philosopher of nature and the physicist attain the same science, whereas the metaphysician and the philosopher of nature spend their time in different sciences.

24. *Philosophy of Nature and Physical Science are Species of the Same Genus, but are Generically Different from Metaphysics.* Jacques Maritain[24] and others admit that the philosophy of nature and physical science are different species of knowledge which, however, belong to the same genus—namely, the one that is characterized by the first degree of abstraction. Both types of knowledge of nature differ generically from metaphysics. In a modified form, the difficulty raised against the preceding view can be objected against this position. If philosophy of nature differs only specifically from physical science but generically from metaphysics, there is no reason why the philosopher of nature who lacks training in physics should feel immediately at home in metaphysics, but find himself in totally foreign territory when he switches his attention to physical theories that are supposed to belong to the same general category as the philosophy of nature. Moreover— and this reason applies also against the first-mentioned view—, there is no way in which a theory of the philosophy of nature, e.g., the matter-form thesis, can be verified by a

---

[24]*Philosophy of Nature,* New York, 1951 pp. 89 ff.

return to sense experience, as is demanded by Thomas Aquinas.

25. *Philosophy of Nature is a Metaphysical Study and Differs Essentially from the Experimental Sciences.* Andrew G. van Melsen[25] and others maintain this view and argue that nowadays philosophy of nature is no longer the same as it was in former ages. We cannot continue to disregard the rise of the new sciences or relegate them to the rank of purely technical knowledge. They point out that the old philosophy of nature has been divided into a group of autonomous experimental sciences and a strictly philosophical branch of learning. The typical element of the experimental sciences is precisely their return to sense experience for verification. On the other hand, the problems that still form part of modern philosophy of nature share with metaphysics not only their method and principles but also the characteristic way in which they can be verified by the intellect alone. In other words, instead of laying stress on the level of *abstraction,* we should pay attention to the manner of *verification.*

Accordingly, proponents of this view place modern philosophy of nature on the same level of knowledge as metaphysics itself. It differs from general metaphysics only insofar as it is concerned with the philosophical character of being as it reveals itself in the material world, whereas general metaphysics studies being as such. In support of this view one may even quote St. Thomas himself, for he explicitly admitted that "a science which is concerned with act, with potency, with unity, or anything of the sort could be called a part of metaphysics, because these are considered in the same way as is being which is the subject of metaphysics."[26] It is precisely these questions which

---

[25] *The Philosophy of Nature,* pp. 98 ff.
[26] *In Boethium de Trinitate,* q. V, a.1, ad 6. English translation, p. 15.

have been able to maintain themselves as strictly pertaining to the philosophy of nature. Accordingly, we may say that the philosophical study of nature, as it is done in our time, is essentially the same science as metaphysics.

SUMMARY

26. The question as to what this material world is allows various correct but partial answers. For this reason the reply given by the philosophy of nature is not a substitute for that supplied by experimental science but a complement. It endeavors to evaluate the material world in the light of metaphysics. Empirical sciences can be verified by a return to sense experience. However, it would be arbitrary and even self-contradictory to limit the power of our intellect to conclusions that are experimentally verifiable. The intellect may reach a level of thought in which no sense-perceptible element is retained and therefore no verification by the senses is possible. This level is reached in the philosophy of nature. Its conclusions have to be verified by checking the truth of the experiential starting point and the logical correctness of the argumentation.

The philosophy of nature takes its starting point in sense experience. Although it does not *a priori* exclude the data obtained by experimental science, *de facto* it does not need these data to arrive at its essential insights into the nature of the material world. Pre-scientific experience is sufficient for this purpose. By "pre-scientific" we do not mean "primitive" or incorrect experience, but primary data, which are of such a nature that no subsequent research can jeopardize their validity.

Experimental scientists can help the philosophers of nature negatively by sounding due warning when he unwittingly attempts to invade the realm of science or proceeds too hastily in his conscious efforts to think scien-

tifically. The same applies vice versa. Positively, science
can help the philosophy of nature by supplying examples
that are not based on primitive knowledge of nature, by
opening up new areas in which its fundamental principles
can find an application, and by making it adapt this application to certain physical realities whose exact nature
can be discovered only by means of scientific instruments.

The method of the philosophy of nature is inductive in
gathering the experiential data that constitute its starting
point; it then analyzes them for their philosophical content,
examining them in the light of general metaphysical principles, and drawing its conclusions from the available
evidence. Finally, it tries to proceed further deductively
and arrive at an interconnected whole of statements that
allow a measure of insight into the nature of material
being. This insight is very fundamental and constitutes
an indispensable complement of both general metaphysics
and experimental science in man's quest for integral knowledge of the world.

The distinction between experimental science and philosophy of nature as autonomous branches of knowledge
dates only from modern times. In former ages all theoretical study of nature was called physics or philosophy
of nature. The increasing use of the experimental method
slowly resulted in the rise of the special sciences of nature
and liberated the philosophical study of nature from a
host of theories that were foreign to its character.

Even nowadays there is no agreement as to what philosophy of nature should be. Some consider it as nothing but
a petrifaction of science, a preparatory stage of physical
theories, or a synthesis of the results of science. Others
see room for it only as a positivistic analysis of scientific
propositions, a study of the forms of thinking proper to
science, or a philosophical reflection on the results of science. Among those who admit an autonomous philosophy
of nature, some try to build up a system divorced from

experience (the idealists), others seek for the most fundamental categories of the material world (Nicolai Hartmann), and a third group endeavors to proceed from experience to conclusions that are strictly philosophical. Most philosophers of the Aristotelian-Thomistic tradition belong to this group.

Alongside the philosophy of nature there is room for a philosophical critique of man's knowledge of nature. It evaluates the methods of science and the physical explanations of experience.

St. Thomas distinguished three levels of abstraction corresponding to three different levels of termination (verification) of scientific knowledge. On the first level, he placed "physics" or "philosophy of nature," which is verified by a return to the senses; on the second, mathematics which is verified in the imagination; on the third, metaphysics, whose verification can be made by the intellect alone. Opinions vary as to the value of this division of the sciences for modern times. Among those who want to retain the division the most conservative view considers all theoretical knowledge of nature (both science and philosophy) are one and the same science which is specifically distinct from metaphysics. An intermediate view holds that physical science and the philosophy of nature are two species of the same generic science on the same level of knowledge, but generically distinct from metaphysics. The third view claims that the philosophy of nature is of a metaphysical character and essentially different from experimental science. It can point to the identity of language, methods, and mode of verification in metaphysics and philosophy of nature and their difference from those of experimental science to support its position.

Introduction

SUGGESTED READINGS

27. Henry J. Koren (ed.), *Readings in the Philosophy of Nature,* Westminster, 1958:

   a. WHAT IS THE PHILOSOPHY OF NATURE?
   Richard von Mises, *Science in the Incipient Stage,* pp. 4 f.
   Philipp Frank, *Why Do Scientists and Philosophers Disagree?,* pp. 6 ff.
   A. d'Abro, *The Methodology of Science,* pp. 13 ff.
   Moritz Schlick, *The Task of the Philosophy of Nature,* pp. 19 ff.
   Henry Margenau, *Metaphysics of Natural Science,* pp. 21 ff.
   Arthur Eddington, *Selective Subjectivism,* pp. 21 ff.
   Julius Seiler, *Physical Science as Presupposition to the Philosophy of Nature,* pp. 32 ff.
   Norbert M. Luyten, *The Actual Position of the Traditional Philosophy of Nature,* pp. 37 ff.
   Nicolai Hartmann, *How to Work at Insoluble Problems,* pp. 46 f.

   b. SCIENCE AND PHILOSOPHY
   Jacques Maritain, *Philosophy and Experimental Science,* pp. 50 ff.
   Andrew G. van Melsen, *Science of Nature, Philosophy, and Philosophy of Nature,* pp. 61 ff.
   William H. Kane, *The Nature and Extent of the Philosophy of Nature,* pp. 80 ff.
   Jacques Maritain, *The Philosophy of Nature Differs Specifically from the Natural Sciences,* pp. 83 ff.

25

Andrew G. van Melsen, *Physical Science, the Philosophy of Nature, and the Levels of Abstraction*, pp. 88 ff.

c. HISTORICAL STUDY:

Herman L. Van Breda, *The Historical Growth of the Philosophy of Nature, Positive Physical Science, and the Critique of the Physical Sciences*, pp. 91 ff.

Jacques Maritain, *Science and Wisdom*, New York, 1940, pp. 3-69.

D. Dubarle, *Scientific Humanism and Christian Thought*, London, 1956, ch. 4.

Anthony Standen, *Science is a Sacred Cow*, London, 1952.

Alfred North Whitehead, *Science and the Modern World*, Cambridge, 1925.

Philipp Frank, *Philosophy of Science*, Englewood Cliffs, 1957, Introduction, Chapters I and II.

SECTION ONE

THE NATURE OF MATTER

Three main currents of thought may be distinguished with respect to the philosophical problem regarding the nature of matter. They are called mechanism, dynamism, and hylomorphism. Sometimes elements of dynamism and mechanism are combined into mechanical dynamism or dynamic mechanism, a modern form of which is hylosystemism. In this section we will first turn our attention to hylomorphism. Three chapters will be devoted to the hylomorphic theory: one to investigate its starting point (Chapter II), another to study the nature of matter and form (Chapter III), and the third to a brief discussion of certain data of science and hylomorphism (Chapter IV). In Chapter V we will examine the philosophical claims of dynamism, mechanism, and hylosystemism.

CHAPTER TWO

THE STARTING POINT OF HYLOMORPHISM

1. INTRODUCTION

28. In the present chapter we are not concerned with the general hylomorphic way of thinking that constitutes a part of Aristotle's influence on subsequent thought. Without hesitation, everyone speaks of "form" as a determining element with respect to a determinable substratum in almost any realm. Thus, for instance, we speak of an athlete's form, literary forms, forming one's conscience, forming a corporation, etc. In this loose way hylomorphism is part and parcel of western thought. At present, however, we want to investigate whether hylomorphism is valid as a philosophical theory about the nature of material being.

The term "hylomorphism" is derived from two Greek words, *hylē* (matter) and *morphē* (form), and therefore may be transliterated as the matter-form theory. It holds that every material being is essentially composed of primary matter and a substantial form as its ultimate constituent principles. Originated by Aristotle and perfected by Thomas Aquinas, hylomorphism still constitutes the core of the traditional philosophy of nature. In the past it has often been mistaken for a physical theory, even by its proponents themselves. This situation has led to its rejection in some quarters because of an alleged incompatibility with the data of modern science. However, if the theory is stripped of considerations and functions that are foreign to its nature and presented only as a philosophical answer to a philosophical question, there is no reason why it should be regarded as unsatisfactory. Of course, one could say that he is not interested in such problems. In that case we would have no quarrel with him—if only in practice this professed lack of interest in philosophical problems would be maintained.

Different Opinions. Although Thomistic philosophers agree about the validity of hylomorphism, there is no such unity among them regarding the proper experiential starting point of the theory. Prior to the end of the nineteenth century all its supporters referred, though not exclusively, to the occurrence of substantial change in matter as a valid point of departure. Even nowadays many philosophers still use this starting point, but they approach the matter with considerably more circumspection than their predecessors. Others, however, are not convinced that substantial change can serve for this purpose and have developed different approaches, of which there are some hints in ancient and medieval philosophy.

It would lead us too far afield to examine here all the different types of proofs that have been proposed.[1] We will therefore limit ourselves to two arguments which in our opinion can serve as legitimate proofs of hylomorphism, provided that they be preceded by an explanation of certain metaphysical notions. These arguments are taken from substantial change and from the multiplication of individuals in the same species. In addition, we will point out a difficulty in a new kind of argument which in recent times has found an increasingly favorable reception.

2. THE PROOF FROM SUBSTANTIAL CHANGE

29. Before we can reply to the question whether substantial changes do happen in material beings we must first make clear what we mean by such a change. Abstractly speaking, this is easy enough. One can reply that a

---

[1]The interested reader may find a discussion of the pros and cons of half a dozen proofs in the author's *Readings in the Philosophy of Nature.* See Suggested Readings at the end of this chapter in no. 37.

change is substantial if it produces a body endowed with an essentially different nature. Immediately, however, the question arises as to what makes one nature essentially different from another. Why are certain differences called "accidental" and others "essential"?

The Analogous Nature of "Essence." Usually, the difference between essential and accidental characteristics is illustrated by the example of man. Rationality is essential to man, but the shape of his nose, the color of his hair and similar characteristics are accidental. The constant reference to man when there is question of exemplifying metaphysical notions indicates that man's idea of himself functions as a standard for other realities. Although this situation could hardly be different, it contains the danger that we might lose sight of the analogous nature of metaphysical terms in general and of essence, substance, substantial or accidental change in particular. The analogous character of these concepts implies that their significance diminishes constantly in value when we descend lower and lower on the scale of beings. Ultimately, a stage will be reached where one will no longer be able to distinguish predicates as "essential" or "accidental" precisely because reality no longer offers a basis for making this distinction. Let us illustrate this observation by means of an example.

Hardly anyone will deny that man is essentially different from a piece of rock. Man's typical activities of thinking and willing evidently indicate a nature that differs as greatly from that of a piece of rock as is possible in the material world. A denial of an essential difference in this case would imply that the whole notion of essence is declared meaningless because all essences would be the same.

On the other hand, if I ask whether a butterfly is essentially different from an elephant, the question cannot be answered as readily in an affirmative way, for both have fundamentally the same types of activity. One has first to determine what is meant here by an essential difference.

30

Keeping in mind that the analogous nature of this term implies that its value is much less on the level of mere animals than it is with respect to man, we may find a criterion adapted to this level by resorting to anatomical and physiological structures and similar features of the animal world. For these features make the difference between an elephant and a butterfly significantly more important than that between two varieties of butterflies. They indicate different modes of animal being. Of course, the difference is less than that between man and a piece of rock, but by lowering my standards to fit this level of being, I am still justified in speaking here of an essential difference.

If, next, the question is asked whether iron and copper are essentially different, we again have to diminish the value of the term if it has to find any application at all. Here an essential difference cannot mean more than that various samples of iron constantly interact with their surroundings in a typical way which differs from the typical way of reacting found in the samples of copper. Because this typical way of reacting sets all iron aside from all copper, we may say that iron is essentially distinct from copper.

Finally, if one asks whether a table is essentially different from a stool, the question loses all meaning, for there remains nothing to mark an internal differentiation. All that table and stool refer to is the external purpose assigned to these objects by man. One and the same object could be called a table or a stool according to the use made of it by its owner.

30. *Are there Any Substantial Changes?* Having thus clarified the analogous nature of essential difference, let us have another look at the question whether there are any substantial or essential changes. Evidently, now the query is much easier to answer. We may legitimately point out

31

that the whole of the observable material world is characterized by such changes: human beings come into existence and die; food is assimilated and thereby changed into the body of plants or animals; inorganic matter enters into combinations that give it distinctly new characteristics; etc. Although the value of these changes constantly diminishes, we are justified in calling all of them essential changes because our analogous notion of essence itself decreases in value when we consider changes on a lower level of being than man.

In this way hylomorphism can be said to be based on the experiential datum that substantial changes do take place. Briefly put, beings that can change essentially are composed of matter and form; but bodies can change essentially; therefore they are composed of matter and form. The minor premise was explained above. The major is clear: essential change is not an annihilation followed by a creation but implies a determinable principle (matter) that remains as a substratum and common bond when a new determining principle (form) endows a being with essentially different characteristics.

31. *Must we Retain Hylomorphism?* The remark could be made that if this proof of hylomorphism depends on the constantly lowered value of essential change, the importance of the theory itself also becomes increasingly smaller. While our reply is that we fully agree with this remark, we would like to add that, despite its constantly diminishing value on lower levels of being, enough remains to maintain hylomorphism as a philosophical theory which applies to all matter. If we do not accept the matter-form composition of inanimate material beings, we would have to deny that they can undergo a substantial change. Consequently, nutrition, generation, death, and similar phenomena of the living world in which non-living matter is changed into living matter or vice versa, could not be

substantial changes. Thus we would have to admit that plants and animals are not essentially different from non-living bodies. Likewise, there would be no possibility of maintaining hylomorphism with respect to man. When through nutrition matter becomes a part of a human body, it would remain the same essentially unchangeable matter it was before it entered his body. Consequently, man's spiritual ego and his body could not constitute together a single being, but at most there would be an accidental bond: man would be a spirit using a body. But in our consciousness of our own ego we are aware of ourselves as a unit, one being, of which the body is a constituent part. Accordingly, the hylomorphism of the inanimate world is intimately connected with the body-soul unity of man. It cannot be rejected without putting man's unity in jeopardy.

3. THE MULTIPLICATION OF INDIVIDUALS IN THE SAME SPECIES

32. What is meant here by "species" has already been explained in the preceding section, where we stressed that the value of this term is analogous and therefore constantly diminishes in importance when we descend lower on the scale of beings. The other metaphysical notion that needs to be explained here is the term "individual."

33. *The Analogy of the Term "Individual."* Abstractly considered, the individual is described as "undivided in itself but divided from everything else." However, before we can say that there are many individual bodies having the same specific nature, this abstract reply has to be given a more concrete content. In other words, we will first have to answer the question: How are we to distinguish one material individual from another?

33

Here again, we should keep in mind that man functions as the source from which the content of our concept of individual is primarily drawn. A human individual is clearly set apart from other human individual because he is aware of himself as the subject of spiritual and free activities that cannot be attributed to others but are his and his alone. These activities are centered on their subject insofar as they tend to render it more perfect. A relatively fixed, temporally and spatially coherent portion of matter—the human body—is reserved to serve as the material substratum of this center of self-directed activities which through the cooperation of all its parts manages to maintain itself in space and time as distinct from everything else. In this way man is set part from the rest of the world as a distinct whole and individual being.

No such sharp distinction divides individuals on the subhuman level. Below man, all activities are encompassed by matter. Nevertheless, even here we may find something analogously similar to man's individuality. An animal, too, functions, at least to a certain extent, as a temporally and spatially coherent center of self-directed activities that is distinct from other centers and maintains itself as such through the subservience of all its parts to the whole. Although these material activities are governed by non-free inherent patterns, they tend to serve the animal as a distinct unit. The same applies, but again on a lower level, to a plant. It is a temporally and spatially coherent center of activities that are still directed towards dominating its surroundings and maintaining the center as a distinct unit. In this way the plant is still set apart from other similar units.

In the realm of the inorganic, the distinction is reduced to the barest minimum and amounts only to being a relatively fixed, temporally and spatially coherent natural center of interactions with surroundings that are no longer directed towards this center itself. Such a center does not succeed at all in dominating its surroundings. It stands apart from it only in a very minor way—namely, by a relatively closer and more permanent natural[2] cohesion of its various parts. Thus we see that the analogous concept of 'individual'' constantly diminishes in value when it is used on a lower level of being. Nevertheless, enough remains to justify our speaking about different individuals.

33. Species—Individual Structure. In our judgments about material beings we often use such formulas as "Peter is a man" or "this is a rock," thereby indicating two moments of thought: a universal one expressing a mode of being common to a class, and a concrete one that affirms this mode of being of a particular object. The first of these may refer to a class that is considered to be ultimately determined with respect to essential characteristics, i.e., it refers to a species, e.g., man. The second moment indicates that we find these characteristics existing in this or that concrete reality, but not in it alone, but also, at least in principle, in others, for we say "*a* man" and not simply "man," "*a* rock" and not "rock."

The question now is whether this is merely a way of speaking and thinking, a logical structure, or points to a reality, an ontological structure or composition in concrete objects, consisting of a common element (giving rise to "species") and another element limiting the common feature here and now to this or that being (giving rise to the "individual"). Although at first sight one could be inclined to say that there is question here only of a

---

[2]By "natural" cohesion we mean one that arises from an inherent pattern of organization, as e.g. in a crystal. If the cohesion does not result from such a pattern, as for instance in a heap of sand, we do not have to do with an individual body but with an aggregate of individuals. In between these clear-cut examples there is evidently room for borderline cases in which it is difficult to determine whether the object in question is one or more individuals. Cf. no. 58.

logical structure, there is good reason for claiming that this way of thinking is based on an ontological composition.

Hardly anyone will deny that the perfection indicated by "man" is something that exist in reality as a mode of being. But if we can truthfully and in the same sense predicate of Peter and John the mode of being expressed by "man," then neither of these two distinct individuals may be unqualifiedly identified with this mode of being. There must be a principle of diversity in them which makes them different ways of being man. In other words, there is something in Peter which explains why he is "man" and something that accounts for the fact that he is merely "a man." Now that which makes Peter "man" is called *form*, and that which makes him merely "*a man*" is the limiting factor called *matter*. The same line of thought applies to other material beings.

34. *Unity of the Material Principle.* The objection could be raised that this proof does not allow us to conclude to the same "kind" of matter for different species of bodies. All that follows from the line of reasoning pursued by it is that the multiplication of individuals in the same species requires a principle of limitaton or potency with respect to the specific perfection in question, but not that these various principles of limitation are of the same "kind."

It would not do to reply that matter as a purely receptive principle of specific perfection does not have any determinations by which one "kind" can be distinguished from another, so that any attempted differentiation of this matter would imply an internal contradiction. For as a potential principle matter may be and always is defined by the specific perfection to which it refers; consequently, if there are different specific perfections, there can be different matters.[3]

---

[3]As is well-known, St. Thomas admitted a difference between the matters of sublunary and of celestial bodies. The matter of ce-

We therefore think that the validity of this objection cannot be denied. However, we may legitimately ask: Does it invalidate the thesis? The answer will have to be in the negative—whether the potential principle of different kind of material beings is of the same kind or not does not militate against the hylomorphic composition of such beings.

On the other hand, we may ask also: Why should one raise the question whether or not prime matter is the same in all material beings? The only reason appears to lie in the fact that different prime matters would leave substantial changes unexplained. However, once the occurrence of such changes is admitted, there is no difficulty in admitting the sameness of matter in different kind of bodies. All we have to do is to point to these changes as evidence that the material principle of these bodies is potential with respect to all specific forms which can come to actuate it.

*4. THE ARGUMENT FROM TEMPORALITY

35. Some modern authors, such as Fernand Renoirte,[4] argue from the spatio-temporal character of material beings. By this they mean that a material being cannot exist all at once, but has its duration at a particular place and at successive moments. Although the particular place in which it is at a particular moment is accidental, it belongs to the very nature of material being to perdure by existing at successive and mutually exclusive instants. Thus such a being is continuously "becoming," i.e., passing through new successive instants. Now such a "becoming" points to an essential composition. For what is essentially simple

---

lestial bodies was even supposed to be specifically different for each celestial body (Cf. *In I De caelo*, lect. 6, no. 63 in Spiazzi ed.; *In II De caelo*, lect. 16, no. 449). Although his view was based on faulty physics, it shows that he did not reject the idea of different kinds of matter as the recipient principle of specific perfection.

[4] *Cosmology*, New York, 1950, pp. 233 ff.

either is totally what it is or it is not at all, and neither of these two fits material being. Therefore, the material being is essentially composed. On the other hand, it is one being, so that its component "parts" cannot be separate entities, but can only be principles of being. One of them has to account for the fact that the material being has whatever are its definite characteristics, and this is called "substantial form." The other explains why this being is only in a temporally determinable way, and this is called "primary matter."

Critique. Undoubtedly, the spatio-temporal character of bodies is one of the most striking characteristics of material being. The question, however, is whether it can serve as a suitable starting point for the matter-form theory. There are several reasons why this may appear doubtful, but we will limit ourselves here to just one.

Temporality is the opposite of eternity. "Eternal" means that a being is itself totally without any succession whatsoever. Only God is eternal in this way. "Temporal" is any being which is itself only in successive stages. Succession, however, may refer either to the order of activity—namely, in a being that remains essentially the same while acting, or to the very essence of the being in question—namely, in a being that becomes essentially different. In the first case, the succession implies the distinction of subsistent subject and accidental determination (substance and accident), and in the second it points to essential composition (matter and form). To be valid, the argument would have to establish that the second type of succession gives rise to temporality in material being. But this means that it presupposes substantial change.

SUMMARY

36. By hylomorphism we mean the philosophical theory which claims that a body is composed of matter and form as the ultimate constituent principles of its essence.

Hylomorphism may be based on the occurrence of substantial change, i.e., change resulting in a body with an essentially different nature. Keeping in mind that the value of "essential difference" diminishes constantly on levels of being below man, we may say that inanimate bodies are esssentially different if one kind constantly interacts with its surroundings in a way that differs from another kind. Now experience shows that bodies can change from one kind into another, not only through assimilation by living bodies, but also as the result of purely physical or chemical reactions. But essential change implies a determinable principle (matter) that remains as a substratum and common bond when a new determining principle (form) comes to endow a body with essentially different characteristics. Accordingly, bodies are composed of matter and form as their essential constituent principles.

Although the importance of hylomorphism diminishes greatly when we speak of it in relation to the sub-human world because of the analogous value of the term "essence," it cannot be rejected even for the inanimate world without endangering the body-soul unity of man. Man experiences himself as one being of which the body is a constituent part. Because man's body constantly exchanges its material elements with the world around him, we cannot maintain his essential unity unless we admit that matter in being assimilated by his body changes essentially by becoming human. Without the hylomorphism of the material world, man would be a spirit using a body, but not a rational animal.

Hylomorphism may be based also on the multiplication of individuals in the same species. "Individual" is an analogous concept and therefore its value diminishes constantly when we descend lower on the scale of beings. In the realm of the inorganic it means nothing but a relatively fixed and spatially coherent natural center of activity. Individuals of the same species are those centers which show themselves endowed with the same constant pattern of activity. Our judgments about material objects indicate that we think in terms of species and individual, for we speak about them as particular instances of a whole class: "a man," "a stone," "a tree," etc. This logical structure is a sign of a real structure, for it implies that in a true judgment we cannot unqualifiedly identify the perfection of the species with the individual under consideration, but have to admit that the individual is only a particular way of realizing the common perfection. Therefore, there must be in the individual one element that justifies us in predicating the specific perfection of it (form), and another element that accounts for the fact that the perfection is predicated only in a qualified sense, i.e., as one among many (matter). Accordingly, it follows that such individuals are composed of matter and form as their constituent principles.

Although this argument does not allow us to conclude to the same kind of material principle in all bodies, it proves their hylomorphic composition. Matter of the same kind is needed only if bodies can undergo substantial change. Once this kind of change is admitted, we may readily conclude that the material principle of all bodies is of the same "kind."

Temporality which characterizes all matter points to the non-simplicity of the material world. Alone, however, it cannot serve as a basis of hylomorphism, for the succession needed for temporality does not necessarily have to be in the essential order, but may refer to the succession

40

of accidental determinations and therefore point only to the non-simplicity of substance and its accidents.

SUGGESTED READINGS

37. Aristotle, *Physica,* bk. I, chs. 4-9.

Thomas Aquinas, *De principiis naturae; On Being and Essence,* ch. 2; *Comment. in I Physic.,* lect. 12.

Henry J. Koren, *Readings in the Philosophy of Nature:*

a. Substantial Change in Inorganic Matter: *Argument* (Edouard Hugon) ; *Critique* (Andrew G. van Melsen) ; pp. 135 ff.

b. Substantial Change in Living Bodies: *Argument* (Peter Hoenen) ; *Critique* (Fernard Renoirte) ; pp. 141 ff.

c. Extension of Bodies: *Argument* (Pedro Descoqs) ; *Critique* (Peter Hoenen) ; pp. 147 ff.

d. Opposition of Body to Intellectual Being: *Argument* (Vincent Remer) ; *Critique* (Pedro Descoqs) ; pp. 150 ff.

e. Species—Individual Structure of Matter; *Argument* (Andrew van Melsen) ; *Critique* (Peter Hoenen) ; pp. 153 ff.

f. Spatio-Temporal Character of Bodies: *Argument* (Fernand Renoirte) ; *Critique* (Ernan McMullin) ; pp. 166 ff.

J. A. J. Peters, "Matter and Form in Metaphysics," *The New Scholasticism,* vol. 31 (1957), pp. 447-483.

Louis de Raeymaeker, *The Philosophy of Being,* St. Louis, 1954, pp. 155 ff.

Peter Hoenen, *The Philosophical Nature of Physical Bodies,* West Baden Springs, 1955, pp. 1-16.

CHAPTER THREE

MATTER AND FORM

In this chapter we will attempt to determine more accurately the meaning and scope of hylomorphism by a careful study of the nature of matter and form and the consideration of some special problems concerning the substantial form of material bodies.

1. MATTER

38. As was pointed out in the preceding chapter, the prime matter spoken of in philosophy should not be conceived as if it were a being in its own right. It is nothing but a principle of being which together with its co-principle, substantial form, constitutes the essence of a material being and makes intelligible why such a being is subject to substantial change and why its essence can exist in many individuals.

Reality of Prime Matter. Although prime matter is merely a principle of being, it is real. It is not only an object of our intellect, of our consideration, but exists in reality. Of course, it is true that this matter cannot be known to us without being considered. However, in this respect it does not differ from any other reality, for nothing is known unless it is considered. The reason why we must assert the reality of prime matter lies in the fact that substantial change and the multiplication of individuals in the same species belong to the order of reality. They are ontological events and therefore can be explained only by means of an ontological structure—namely, that of matter and form.

42

All material has prime matter + specific perfection

Matter and Form

No Separate Existence. The assertion that prime matter is a real or ontological principle of material being should not be understood to mean that it exists apart from form. Anything that exists or can exist separately has a "to be" of its own or at least is ordered to "to be" as a complete essence. But prime matter is not a complete essence, but merely an essential principle which explains why different substantial perfections can successively come to actuate the same material being and why there can be many individuals endowed with the same specific perfections.

The denial of a separate existence to matter without form should not be taken to mean that prime matter does not exist at all. Just as an essence is real but does not exist separately from its "to be," so also matter is real but does not exist separately from the "to be" that belongs to the composite of matter and form. In other words, the potential principle of a material being never exists in pure potency, but is always actuated by a form. For otherwise it would be a pure potency having the act of being, which is a contradiction in terms.

39. *Prime Matter and Corruption.* Prime matter is the substratum which remains throughout all successive changes and serves as their common bond. It itself is not subject to substantial changes, i.e., generation or corruption, for it is not a substance but only a substantial principle. It is the composite of prime matter and form that can change substantially.

Despite its own incorruptibility, prime matter is the principle of corruption in material beings. The reason lies in the potential character of prime matter. Being in potency to any substantial form that can come to actuate it, matter is never actuated to the fullness of its capacity. While actuated by one form, it is deprived of the others. Thus this constant state of privation may be considered as an external and negative principle from which substantial

43

change arises—external in the sense that privation itself does not enter the new composite as one of its constituent principles.

Knowability of Prime Matter. It should be noted that just as prime matter cannot exist separately from form, so also it cannot be known separately from its relation to form. Being purely potential, it lacks any determination by which it could be known. As Aristotle expressed it in his famous definition: It "is of itself neither a particular thing, nor of a particular quantity, nor otherwise positively characterized."[1]

Nevertheless, prime matter is knowable insofar as by its very nature it is related to form as the co-principle of essence. This transcendental relationship[2] of matter to form makes it possible for us to describe prime matter as the limiting and receptive constituent principle of a body's essence.

The nature of prime matter may perhaps be more easily understood by means of an analogy. A ball of modeling clay may successively be given different forms, but none of these forms is to be identified with the clay. The clay is never without a form, but no matter what form it actually has, it remains capable of subsequently receiving others.[3] So also prime matter is not to be identified with substantial form, although it is never without such a form; moreover, whatever form it has, it remains potential with respect to others. Evidently, modeling clay is not an example of prime matter, for modeling clay possesses already the form of being clay, but merely serves here as a comparison. It may be called *secondary* matter, inasmuch as it can retain its nature of clay while undergoing accidental modification.

---

[1] *Metaphysics,* bk. VII, ch. 3; 1029a 23.
[2] Concerning the nature of transcendental relations, see the author's *Metaphysics,* pp. 217 f.
[3] Cf. Aristotle, *Physics,* bk. I, ch. 7; 191a 7, and St. Thomas commentary on this text.

2. FORM

40. Some of the assertions made with respect to matter apply in a modified way also to the purely material form.[4] They are the following:

a. Form is not a being in its own right but merely a *principle of being* which together with matter constitutes the essence of a body.

b. Form is *real*. It is admitted in order to explain the ontological structure of essentially mutable beings and the ontological multiplicity of specifically the same essential perfection. Evidently, these ontological data can be explained only by means of ontological or real principles.

c. Although the purely material form is real, it *does not exist separately* from matter. It is not a being, but merely a principle of being which together with its co-principle matter constitutes the essence of the material reality that exists.

d. Because the substantial form confers on the physical body which it co-constitutes its primary or essential perfection, it is correctly described as the *first act of a physical body,* i.e., as the perfecting or determining essential principle of a material substance.

3. THE ORIGIN OF THE MATERIAL FORM

41. Where does the new substantial form come from when a body undergoes an essential change?

No Direct Generation. First of all, it is to be noted that the form cannot come to be directly or separately (*per se*). Coming to be must be proportionate to the "to be" to which

---

[4]By purely material form we mean a form whose operations and nature are totally encompassed by matter. It does not have any activity that is intrinsically independent of matter. The only form of matter which is not purely material is the human soul. Cf. the author's *Animate Nature,* ch. XVIII.

it leads. But, as we have seen, the form does not exist separately; therefore, it cannot come to be separately. There can be question of its coming to be only insofar as the composite of which it constitutes the determining principle comes to be.

Misunderstanding of this point has often resulted in the rejection of hylomorphism itself. Once the form is considered as a being in its own right and not merely as a principle of being, its origin can be explained only as an infusion from without as a result of a creative act. Understandable reluctance to admit such a creation wherever there would be question of essential change caused Descartes and others to abandon hylomorphism entirely.

Although a substantial form does not come to be directly, nevertheless *somehow* it comes to be when a substantial change takes place, i.e., prior to the change, it neither existed separately nor actuated matter. It is therefore legitimate to raise the question how it comes to be.

It would not do to reply that the new form was concealed in matter before the change and that change merely draws it from its hiding place. For a form that would be merely concealed would actually exist, and therefore before the change it would be either an actuality of matter or have a separate existence. But both of these alternatives must be excluded: if it already actuated matter there would be no change and if, on the other hand, it could exist separately it would not be a purely material form, for it would exist independently of matter.

42. *Eduction of Form.* The only coming to be of which there can be question with respect to a new substantial form in the process of essential change is its coming to be actual, i.e., its passing from being-in-potency to being-in-act. When we say that prime matter is capable of being actuated successively by many forms, we express equivalently that many forms are in the potency of matter. Under

the influence of the external agent which causes a body to change essentially, one of these forms begins to actuate matter. Thus matter is reduced from potency to act with respect to this form. Looking upon this reduction from the viewpoint of the new form, we may say that, as the technical formula expresses it, the form is educed from the potency of matter.[5]

In this way it becomes clear how the solution of Parmenides' dilemma[6] shows how the problem of the form's origin should be solved. Prior to the change, the new form is neither simply non-being nor being. The change means the transition from being-in-potency to being-in-act with respect to the new essential perfection. Before the change, this perfection or form is potentially in matter, and when the change takes place, it comes to be actually.

It may not be amiss to point out that the potential existence of form is not something that can be represented by our imagination. Any attempt to imagine a potential form can end only in the idea of the form being concealed in matter and gives rise to the difficulties that were mentioned above. The point that has to be kept in mind all the time with respect to form is that form is not a being but merely a principle of being and therefore has to be treated as such.

4. THE "ULTIMATE DISPOSITION"

43. As we have seen above, matter is potential with respect to all substantial forms and can be successively informed by many. When under the influence of an external agent a substantial change takes place, the old form is reduced to potency and a new one comes to actuate matter. To cause this transition the agent must act upon the material subject and render it unsuitable for continued

---

[5]The term "educed" is used here to indicate that this form is not introduced from without, but comes from the potentiality of matter.
[6]Concerning this dilemma see the author's *Metaphysics,* nos. 114 ff.

actuation by its present form. As experience shows, a substance can undergo a certain amount of modification without becoming essentially different. Water, for example, can undergo certain modifications, e.g., in pressure, without being resolved into hydrogen and oxygen. For the sake of illustrating the point at issue more easily, let us assume that water and ice are essentially different. Experience shows that the temperature can be varied to some extent without causing the water to become ice. With respect to substantial change, such accidental qualities as temperature and pressure are called the "dispositions" of the substance. Thus we may say that certain modifications of a substance are possible without resulting in an essential change. To revert to our example, as the temperature of the water continues to drop, the disposition (the temperature) of the subject matter becomes less and less compatible with its nature of being water, until finally the last degree is reached at which water can remain water. This last degree of temperature—and the same applies also to other dispositions—which is compatible with being-water is technically called the *ultimate disposition* prior to the substantial change of water into ice.[7] The reason is that, if the cooling agent persists in acting upon it, the water becomes ice, i.e., it loses its substantial form of water and comes to be actuated by that of ice. The first disposition (temperature) of the new substance (ice) is the same as that of the old one (water). However, this sameness is one of degree (32°F) only, but not of individual identity, for the subjects of both are different.[8]

Priority of Disposition to Substance. It is to be noted that this first disposition is both prior and not prior to the new substance. It is prior to it in the genus of material

---

[7]Cf. P. Hoenen, *Cosmologia,* Nota XIX, 4th ed., Rome 1949, pp. 556 ff.

[8]As accidents, these dispositions are individuated by their subjects. Cf. the author's *Metaphysics,* no. 212.

causality, for it prepares the subject matter for substantial change. On the other hand, it is posterior to it in the genus of formal causality, for as an accident it needs to inhere in a substantial subject. This priority and posteriority, however, is not one of time but only of nature.[9] With respect to time, the new substance and its dispositions are simultaneous, for cause and effect are simultaneous. The only priority of which there is question here is that of nature: as a disposition for a new substantial form, the accidental modification preceded this form, but as an accident it follows it. Thus we have here an example of the interaction of causes, i.e., causes causing one another, that was spoken of in general metaphysics.[10]

44. *An Objection.* The objection could be raised that accidental dispositions cannot give rise to a substantial change because cause and effect must be proportionate to each other. Although at first sight this objection may seem to be grave, it can easily be disposed of. All we have to keep in mind here is that a substance is not an inert support but a dynamic reality which acts by means of its accidental qualities.[11] Thus these accidents are like instruments of a substance and therefore share in the causality that is proper to the substantial agent. They do not act as independent entities but through them the substance acts. Therefore, they can bring about a modification on the substantial level of being, for the effect of an instrument is proportionate to the principal agent.

5. Unicity of Substantial Form in a Single Body

45. Does a single body contain two or more substantial forms or only one? By "single body" we mean here an

---

[9]Concerning priority of time and of nature, cf. *op. cit.,* no. 228.
[10]Cf. *op. cit.,* no. 265.
[11]Cf. *Animate Nature,* no. 43.

essentially unified material whole as distinct from an aggregate such as a pile of bricks. The answer to this question flows from the very nature and function of substantial form.

The substantial form makes prime matter pass from being-in-potency to being-in-act with respect to substantial perfection by making the composite this or that determined substance. Once this transition is effected, the subject is no longer potential with respect to substantial being but actually is a substance, and a substance of this or that nature as long as the substantial form in question actuates prime matter. Therefore, it would be impossible for another substantial form to actuate the prime matter together with the first form, for the matter is no longer potential with respect to substantial being.

Or to say it somewhat differently, two substantial forms in the same body would mean that two acts of the same order actuate one potency. This is impossible because once a potency is actuated it is no longer potency.

Again, if two or more substantial forms actuated matter at the same time, the composite would have to be this kind of a substance by virtue of the first form, and simultaneously a different kind by virtue of the other form, which is impossible.

"Subordinate" Forms. One could object that this argument does not hold for substantial forms which are subordinated to one another. Why, for instance, should it be impossible for one form to make matter a body and for another to make it, say, iron? The reply is that we must distinguish the logical subordination of essential perfections from the ontological principles from which these perfections may spring. In distinct beings that differ essentially substantial perfections can be accounted for by distinct ontological principles or forms which can be arranged according to a scale of decreasing values or subordination.

50

However, if a single being possesses a plurality of essential perfections corresponding to distinct forms in different beings, we cannot admit in it a plurality of substantial forms. The reason is that a substantial form is an ontological principle which actuates the potential element of the body in question with respect to its substantial being and, once this potentiality is actuated, any other form added to it would accrue to something that is already constituted as a substantial being; hence such a form could be only an accidental perfection or a secondary determination.

46. *Virtual Plurality.* Although these reasons compel us to deny the possibility of two or more substantial forms simultaneously actuating the same matter, it may be admitted that a single substantial form is *virtually* many insofar as in a being of a higher rank the form is the ontological principle of perfections which in distinct lower beings stem from different substantial forms. For instance, the human soul alone is the source of man's essential perfections in their entirety, although some of these perfections are found on levels below man, and on these levels derive their origin from different substantial forms. In this way man's soul is virtually equivalent to the substantial forms of body, organism, and animal, but formally speaking it is only one form.

6. Substantial Forms in "Immediate Potency"

47. Although in principle prime matter is potential with respect to any substantial form, experience shows that in many cases the dissolution of a body produces certain kinds of substances rather than others. Thus, for instance, when water is dissolved, whether by means of an electric current, chemical means, or heat, it decomposes into hydrogen and oxygen. Philosophically speaking, this means that the dissolution of water results in the eduction of the substantial forms of hydrogen and oxygen and not

those of any other substances. What is the reason for the constant recurrence of these forms in preference to others?

The irrelevance of the kind of agent causing the change shows that this phenomenon must be attributed not so much to the agent as to the material conditions under which water exists. These dispositions are such that the substantial forms of hydrogen and oxygen do not exist in the same state of pure potentiality as the forms of other substances into which water cannot be changed so easily. The qualities or dispositions of water are more closely related to those of its composing elements than to other substances. Accordingly, we may say that its prime matter is closer to actuation by the forms of hydrogen and oxygen than by those of other substances.

If it is permissible to use an analogy here, we may say that just as a steel spring that is bent into a circular form is closer to being elliptical than straight, so also prime matter, as actuated by one form, may be more immediately disposed to some forms than to others. For this reason the new substantial forms most readily following on the old form are said to be present not in a remotely potential way but by way of immediate potency.

7. UNION OF MATTER AND FORM

48. The question of union of matter and form was considered already within the framework of general metaphysics.[12] It may be useful, however, to repeat here the answer given to this question. Whenever two or more separately existing things have to be united there is need for a principle of union that is distinct from these things. Thus, for instance, if we want to join two pieces of iron, we have to use bolts or weld them together. The reason is that the two pieces exist as beings in their own right, at least prior to the union. But it would be meaningless

---

[12]Cf. *Metaphysics* no. 152. See also no. 127.

to raise the question of a common bond with respect to mere principles of being. Such principles are not beings, but merely the constituent elements of a single being which alone exists. They do not have a "to be" of their own but are only insofar as form actuates matter. Consequently, the union of matter and form can have no other meaning than that matter is actuated by form. For this reason it is said that matter and form are united by their very nature and not by means of a third intrinsic principle or bond, for it is the very nature of form to actuate matter.

To express the same idea differently, unity is consequent on being, for unity or oneness is a transcendental property of being.[13] Now matter and form constitute a being only insofar as form actuates matter. Therefore, they are united or "one" by their very nature.

*8. HISTORICAL NOTES

49. Prior to St. Thomas, many medieval philosophers, such as *Alexander of Hales* († 1245) and *St. Bonaventure* (1221-1274), admitted universal hylomorphism,[14] i.e., the matter-form composition of all finite beings, including purely spiritual beings, although in spirits matter was not supposed to be "corporeal." *St. Thomas'* vigorous insistence on corruptibility as the primary reason for hylomorphism, and the role he assigned to the real distinction between essence and "to be" in finite beings gradually caused the extension of matter-form composition to spiritual creatures to be abandoned.

The pure potentiality of matter was denied by *Duns Scotus* (1270-1308) and others who denied the real distinction of essence and "to be." Francis Suarez (1548-1617) held a somewhat ambiguous position, for he called

---

[13]Cf. *op. cit.*, nos. 68 f.
[14]Cf. Patrice Robert, *L'hylémorphisme universel au XIII siècle,* Quebec, 1953.

matter pure potency but attributed to it a kind of actual existence.

Regarding the origin of substantial forms, the tendency to conceive form as a being rather than as a mere principle of being caused some Arabian philosophers to have recourse to creation. Reluctance to appeal to creation induced *Descartes* and others to reject hylomorphism entirely.

A plurality of substantial forms in a single being was admitted by *Avicebron* (c. 1021-c. 1058), followed by many other medieval philosophers, such as *Scotus* and *St. Bonaventure* (1221-1274), although they varied in their explanation of this plurality. In the earlier works of *St. Thomas* there are a few texts that show traces of a special form of corporeity, but very soon he resolutely defended the unicity of the substantial form in a single being. As is well known, at first his view was censured by the Bishops of Paris and Canterbury (1277), but better understanding of his position quickly prevailed and caused its acceptance by all except the Scotists. In more recent times, *Pedro Descoqs,* who also quotes *Tilman Pesch, Donat* and others in his favor, reverted to a pluralism of forms because of certain difficulties thought to arise from the atomic theory.[15]

The immediate union of matter and form was rejected by *Scotus,* who required a common bond distinct from both. *Suarez* tried to establish the union by means of a substantial mode. The nominalists (William of Ockham, †1349?) saw the unifying element in the mere togetherness (*indistantia*) of matter and form.

SUMMARY

50. Although matter is not a being in its own right but merely a principle of being, it is real, for the ontological

---

[15]Cf. below, no. 62.

realities of substantial change and multiplication of individuals in the same species require an ontological and not a purely logical principle of explanation.

As a mere principle of being, prime matter cannot exist separately or in a pure state, but only as actuated by form in the matter-form composite. Prime matter itself is not subject to substantial change (for it is not composed), but it makes the composite changeable insofar as no form actuates it to the fullness of its capacity.

Because of its purely potential character, matter cannot be known except insofar as it is related to its determining co-principle or form.

Like matter, the purely material form is merely a principle of being. It is real, but does not exist separately for the same reason that matter is real and does not exist separately.

The material form does not come to be directly but only indirectly insofar as the composite of which it is a component part comes to be. Its coming to be consists in its passing from potency to act as the determining principle of the new composite, i.e., its eduction from the potency of matter.

This transition from potency to act is brought about when an external agent continues to modify the dispositions of a body which has reached the ultimate dispositions compatible with its present nature. In this case these ultimate dispositions become the first dispositons of the new substance. Although these dispositions are accidental qualities, they can produce a substantial change insofar as they are instruments of a substantial agent.

A substantially unified body has only one substantial form, for matter is related to form as potency is to act. Once matter is actuated in the substantial order, it is no longer in potency to substantial being, so that any added form can give the composite only a secondary or accidental mode of being. However, a substantial form may be called virtually many insofar as it confers a plurality of perfections on its subject.

A substantial form is said to be present in immediate potency if prime matter, as actuated by its present form, is immediately disposed to be actuated by this other form.

Prime matter and substantial form unite of themselves, without any intermediary common bond, because it is the very nature of form to actuate matter. A common bond would be needed only if there were question of uniting two beings, but is not needed for mere principles of being.

SUGGESTED READINGS

51. Aristotle, *Physica,* bk. I; *Metaphysica,* bk. VII, chs. 3, 7 and 8.

Thomas Aquinas, *Comment. in I Physic.,* lect. 11-14; *in VII Metaphysics.,* lect. 7, *in VIII Metaphysic.,* lect. 1; *De principiis naturae; On Being and Essence,* ch. 2; *Summa theol.,* p. I, q. 65, a. 4 and q. 66, a. 1; *On the Power of God,* q. 3, a. 8.

Henry J. Koren, *Readings in the Philosophy of Nature:*

Dermot O'Donoghue, *Aristotle's Doctrine of "The Underlying Matter,"* pp. 176 ff.

John O'Neill, *Substantial Form,* pp. 180 ff.

Selected Passages from Aristotle and Thomas Aquinas, pp. 185 ff.

Peter Hoenen, *The Virtual Presence of Elemental Forms in the Compound,* pp. 191 ff.

Peter Hoenen, *The Philosophical Nature of Physical Bodies,* West Baden Springs, 1955, pp. 21-73.

CHAPTER FOUR

HYLOMORPHISM AND SOME DATA OF SCIENCE

In this chapter we will consider some scientific data which sometimes are brought to bear against the matter-form composition of matter.

1. THE DISCONTINUITY OF MATTER

52. According to science, a molecule is composed of atoms in which one or more electrons move at a distance around a nucleus. Therefore, matter is discontinuous. But it is impossible for a single substantial form to actuate particles of matter that are not continuous, for the form would have to act over empty space, i.e., at a distance,[1] which is impossible. Thus one would have to admit that each subatomic particle has its own substantial form.

Regarding this line of reasoning the following points need to be observed:

1. The argument does not prove anything at all against hylomorphism as such, but, if valid, would merely reject the substantial unity of bodies larger than these particles.

2. The difficulty enunciated by the argument would affect not only the philosophical problem of how a substantial form can exercise its influence on supposedly discontinuous matter, but applies with equal force against any type of physical action between particles. Therefore, if this objection disproves the substantial unity of bodies larger than the smallest particles, it will also force us to abandon the reality of all physical and chemical reactions.

---

[1]Concerning the impossibility of action at a distance, see no. 64.

3. The above-mentioned discontinuity exists not only in the sub-atomic world, but also in the realm of the living. Nevertheless, man experiences himself as a single being and not as an aggregate of billions of autonomously existing things.

These last two remarks show that there must be something wrong with the argument. Its mistake lies in the hidden transition from the discontinuity of particles having *mass* to the discontinuity of all matter. From the fact that nothing having mass ("rest mass") is observable between particles we may not conclude that no matter at all extends between them. The electromagnetic and gravitational fields which, according to science, surround all bodies imply the existence of a material medium. For this reason the nucleus and its surrounding electrons do not have to be conceived as separated by space devoid of all matter. To say it differently, the particles in question are not a total representation of material reality, but only a partial picture of it in terms of a mechanical model.

Moreover, there is another point that should be kept in mind when one speaks of the action of a substantial form. When scientists and philosophers deny the possibility or at least the occurrence of action at a distance, they are concerned with efficient causality. But the very term "action" does not apply in a strict sense to the influence of a formal cause. A substantial form does not act but *actuates*, i.e., it is the internal organizing principle of a material being, and exercises its causality by its very nature. Thus there appears to be no reason why the above-mentioned spatial discontinuity of particles and the impossibility of acting at a distance should militate against their incorporation into a more complex unit.

2. Transformation of Matter into Energy

53. In nuclear fission the mass of the resulting parts is not equal to that of the original atom but about 0.1%

smaller. This "mass defect" is accounted for by the release of an enormous amount of energy (about thirty million kilowatt hours for a single gram of matter or the power produced by 2000 locomotives during one hour). Physicists sometimes refer to this phenomenon as the transformation of matter into energy.

Does this transformation contradict the hylomorphic constitution of matter? At first sight, it may appear so, for if the term "matter" is taken at its face value it would mean that a material substance (matter) is changed Into an accident (energy). Evidently, if matter can be transformed into energy, it cannot be a substance and consequently the philosophical assertion that a material substance is composed of the two substantial principles of matter and form will be meaningless.

However, when scientists speak about the transformation of matter into energy or vice versa, they unwittingly identify the substance of *matter* with its accident of *mass*.[2] This identification seems to flow from the tacit assumption that the essence of matter consists in its measurable aspects. It does not have a foundation in science itself. Accordingly, we must reject the claim that the transformation of "matter" into energy proves anything against hylomorphism.

3. FUNDAMENTAL UNITY OF MATTER

54. When a stream of neutrons is directed against silver, radioactivity occurs and the silver is changed into cadmium. A similar stream causes uranium to fall apart into barium and krypton. Although man has not yet succeeded in transforming all elements into one another, theoretically it appears possible that such a transformation can be effected. This phenomenon indicates the fundamental unity of matter and is in agreement with

---

[2]Concerning the meaning of mass, see below, no. 77.

the philosophical view that all bodies are composed of the same "kind" of prime matter and different substantial forms.

Elements consist of a nucleus and a variable number of electrons—the exact number of which is indicated by the atomic number assigned to each in the periodic table. Accordingly, the difference between various elements appears to arise from the diversity of their number of electrons. Thus perhaps one would ask whether we may identify the form with the electrons and prime matter with the nucleus.

The reply is that any such identification would be wholly out of place. Both nucleus and electrons are material particles constituting an atom. Their existence merely indicates that an atom is not homogeneous but heterogeneous matter. Each of these particles has a hylomorphic constitution. This, however, does not mean that every particle has its own substantial form. Like any material part that enters into combination with others to constitute a larger substantially unified whole, these particles are informed by the substantial form of the whole. On the other hand, if any particle is expelled from the whole, as happens in radioactivity, it has its own substantial form as long as it continues to exist separately from a larger unit of matter.[3]

4. UNICITY OF SUBSTANTIAL FORM

55. *Permanence of Atoms in Compound.* The unicity of the substantial form in units of matter larger than the atom is sometimes attacked on the following grounds:

If a chemical compound is analysed by means of X-rays, it produces the typical spectra of the elements of which it is composed. Therefore, this spectrum shows that the ele-

---

[3]Cf. below, no. 58.

ments continue actually to exist in the compound so that molecules and *a fortiori* larger units of matter are mere aggregates without substantial unity.

The same seems to follow from the phenomenon that radioactive elements which enter into a chemical compound continue to produce radiation. Since action follows being, one would have to say that if these elements still act in the compound, then they still exist. Consequently, the compound would be a mere aggregate.

In reply, we may point out, first of all, that it is very questionable whether a chemical compound remains intact under X-ray analysis. The molecules emitting the spectrum are subjected to an intense bombardment of rays and it is not likely that they can withstand the attack without being resolved into their components. Thus it is not surprising if only the spectra of the elements appear.[4]

However, let us suppose that the compound does not dissolve under the X-ray analysis. The available evidence in that case does not allow us to conclude that the atoms exist *actually* in the compound. Such an actual existence would imply that the atoms themselves are the ultimate subjects of the radiation. Although this statement may be true with respect to separately existing atoms, it would have to be proved for atoms that have entered into combination with others. But the persistence of the X-ray spectrum can be explained also if some of the activities proper to the atom remain in the compound as activities whose ultimate subject is the compound. If the atoms were to lose all their characteristic qualities when they enter into composition, they could not make any specific contribution to the resultant whole. Consequently, the nature of a compound would bear no relationship to that of the atoms of which it was composed. This, however, is obviously against experience. Thus we may conclude that these atoms contribute some of their properties to the compound,

4Cf. Hoenen, *Cosmologia,* no. 309.

i.e., some qualities remain the same,[5] although they do no longer belong to the atom as to their ultimate subject, but to the compound of which the atoms are physically constituent parts. As was mentioned before, the permanence of these qualities may be expressed by saying that the atoms continue to exist *virtually*.[6]

The same reply may be given with respect to the permanence of radio-activity when a radioactive element become a part of a chemical compound.

56. *Impurity of Material Substances.* Another difficulty against the unicity of substantial form arises in units of matter that are larger than a single molecule. Although theoretically it is possible to classify matter as iron, gold, silver, etc., in practice a piece of matter is always impure and contains traces of "foreign" matter. On the other hand, we want to consider any body that shows a close natural cohesion as a single substance.[7] Let us suppose that we have a chunk of metal which contains iron, tin and aluminum. If it is considered as a single substance, one could not claim that its substantial form is that of iron, for it contains also tin and aluminum. Accordingly, either there are no substantial units of matter larger than a molecule or a single substance may have more than one substantial form.

At first sight, this objection may seem to be irrefutable.[8] On closer inspection, however, it appears that an idealized conception of reality plays too important a role. Theo-

---

[5]This sameness is specific but not numerical, for any accident is individuated by its subject; hence a change in subject implies a numerical change. Cf. the author's *Metaphysics,* no. 212.

[6]Physically the permanence of the X-ray spectrum, radioactivity, and other smiliar phenomena is explained by the fact that these activities do not result from the outer shell of the combining atoms but from their inner regions which remain untouched by chemical composition.

[7]Cf. above, no. 32.

[8]Cf. Andrew G. van Melsen, *The Philosophy of Nature,* pp. 146 ff.

retically we may be able to classify matter neatly into specifically distinct categories, and theoretically again the philosopher would admit specifically distinct substantial forms for these different kinds of matter. But if experience shows that these theoretical divisions are idealizations and do not entirely correspond with reality as it exists concretely, then obviously we will have to adopt the application of our philosophical principles to the world as it really is. If a chunk of matter does not really have a single organization pattern allowing us to classify it unqualifiedly as iron and calling for the substantial form of iron, but combines several patterns into a single natural unit, then the substantial form of this unit will not correspond to the specific pattern of iron, but to as many patterns as exist in this unit, for the substantial form makes the unit to be what it really is.

Although this reply may displease man's persistent tendency to classify everything in neatly separate pigeonholes, there appears to be no philosophical reason why a single substantial form could not in different parts of one body give rise to different properties and thus make one part of it "iron" and another "tin" or "aluminum." Thus we may not be able to classify such a form as that of iron and even be at a loss as to how to classify it at all, but this fact merely proves that reality is too complex to be divided by airtight compartments.

One could further object that this line of reasoning obliterates the distinction between substantial unit and aggregate, for an aggregate also could be conceived as a single unit whose various parts are actuated in a different way by one substantial form. The reply is that the distinction between substantial unit and aggregate is not based on the homogeneous or heterogeneous nature of the component parts, but on the absence of natural cohesion that typifies the aggregate. A heap of pellets composed of pure iron remains an aggregate, but a body composed of such a variety of heterogeneous elements as a plant is a single substance.

5. INDIVIDUAL MATERIAL SUBSTANCES

The two extremes with respect to the multiplication of individuals in the realm of matter are, on the one hand, the view that the whole universe together constitutes a single individual substance and, on the other, the position that each material particle is such a substance in its own right.

57. *The Universe as a Single Individual Substance.* The first of these two views presents itself with a charming simplicity. In one stroke it disposes of all problems about the criterion for distinguishing one individual from another. It simply denies any degree of autonomy to the various "parts" of the universe and holds them to be nothing but integral parts of a single subsistent subject.

Unfortunately, there is an unsurmountable difficulty in this view—namely, man's presence in this universe. We cannot escape from the fact that man is set apart from the rest of the universe as a distinct subject which cannot simply be reduced to being just a "part" of a greater whole. For man is aware of himself as distinct from everything that is non-Ego and as the subject of actions that belong to him and to him alone. Thus it becomes apparent that we cannot consider the whole universe as a single substantially unified being.

If the view is moderated somewhat and limited to considering the whole non-human world as a single individual substance, one cannot apodictically show that such a conception is absurd. This absence of absurdity, however, alone is not sufficient to accord the view a degree of plausibility. One would have to find a reason why, alongside the more than two billion human individual substances, the rest of the universe should be considered as a single massive substantial unit. The only reason would seem to be that a further distinction into separate individual substances cannot be made because there is no adequate criterion for distinguishing one substantial unit from another. While man's spiritual nature sets him sharply apart from the rest of the world, the element of spiritual activities is lacking in the non-human universe; consequently, there would seem to be no basis for a further distinction into separate substantial units.

However, this answer allows us only to conclude that the non-human world cannot be divided into substantial individuals of a *human* nature. It fails to take into consideration that the search for such units will have to pay attention to the diminishing value of the term "substantial unit" or "individual substance" when there is question of reality below man. Like any truly metaphysical concept, "individual substance" is an analogous term and therefore has to be dehumanized, i.e., emptied of its specifically human content, when we want to consider its predicability of non-human beings. As was pointed out in Chapter III, this strictly philosophical procedure allows us to retain a certain minimum of autonomous existence in the non-human. We characterized it as the temporal and spatial cohesion resulting from an inherent organization pattern. Undoubtedly, certain "parts" of the universe are characterized by such a cohesion. For this reason we cannot accept the view that the whole of the non-human world constitutes a single individual substance.

58. *Is Each Particle a Distinct Individual Substance?*
Must we, then, go to the opposite extreme and admit that each particle of matter is a distinct individual substance? And if the answer is in the negative, where are we concretely to draw the line between individual substances and mere parts of larger substantial units?

Regarding the many *subatomic particles* discovered by modern science, e.g., electrons, protons, neutrons and positrons, it must be pointed out that these particles and their properties can be understood only within the framework of the larger physical structure (the atom) of which they are parts.[9] Now it is typical of individual substances constituting a mere aggregate that each can be understood on its own, independently of the aggregate. Thus it follows that these subatomic particles, as constituent elements of an atom, are not individual substances. Moreover, the continuity aspect of matter prevails so strongly on the subatomic level that it is almost meaningless to speak of individuality with respect to such particles.[10] However, during the ephemeral existence some particles have outside the atom, it may be legitimate to consider them as distinct individual substances.

What about the *atoms* themselves? Below the molecular level,[11] they do not exist naturally in a separate way, but tend to enter into composition with other atoms and thus constitute a molecule. Although an atom can exist separately and as such may be considered an individual body in its own right, its tendency to unite with others into larger units having a fixed pattern of organization indicates that such an individual existence is not normal for it. It, too, therefore, should be considered as a constituent part of an individual body rather than as an autonomous individual substance.

Are *molecules* the only subsisting individuals of the non-living world or do they lose their actual autonomous

---

[9]Cf. van Melsen, *The Philosophy of Nature,* pp. 212 f.

[10]Cf. Louis de Broglie, "Continuity and Individuality in Modern Physics," *Matter and Light,* Dover Publications, n.d., pp. 217 ff.; E. Schrödinger, "What is an Elementary Particle?" *Endeavour,* vol. 9, July 1950.

[11]A molecule may be monatomic (helium) or polyatomic (hydrogen) according as it consists of one or more atoms.

existence when they constitute larger units of matter? The following answer could be given to this question:

1. Isolated molecules should be considered as distinct individuals.

2. Molecules that constitute a larger unit of matter sometimes retain their autonomous existence and at other times become mere parts of a larger whole according as the whole is a mere aggregate or a single substance. The criterion for distinguishing one from the other was indicated above—if the whole reveals a natural cohesion in space and time, then the molecules are merely parts of a larger unit which is the only actual individual.

Concretely speaking, such a cohesion seems to be lacking in gases and liquids. For this reason we can justifiably say that in these states of aggregation each molecule is a distinct individual substance. In solids a natural cohesion shows itself e.g. in crystals, but is conspicuously lacking in a mere heap of sand. In between these two there are other wholes in which sufficient cohesion is discernible to speak about a single individual unit constituted by molecules; for instance, pieces of metal or rock that are fused.

However, it is difficult, if not impossible, to indicate more accurately where the boundary line lies between the aggregate of individuals and the substantially unified whole. The reason is that the very notion of individual substance is analogous and constantly diminishes in value. Hence it is not surprising that in the realm of the non-living especially a moment is reached when one has to confess that it is no longer feasible to distinguish the individual substance from the mere aggregate of many individuals.

SUMMARY

59. The discontinuity of subatomic particles should be understood in reference to mass and not as if there is no

matter at all between these particles. Understood in this way, this discontinuity does not militate against the hylomorphic theory. Moreover, the admission of space devoid of all matter between the particles would force us to conceive their interaction as action at a distance, which is impossible. Finally, even if matter were really discontinuous, it would prove nothing against hylomorphism, for the substantial form does not act in the manner of an efficient cause but as an organizing principle whose formal causality is identical with its nature.

The transformation of matter into energy, or vice versa, does not mean that a substance is changed into an accident, or vice versa, but merely that the mass of matter is transformed into energy.

The physical possibility of changing elements into one another harmonizes with the hylomorphic view that all bodies are composed of the same prime matter and different forms which give rise to each body's essential characteristics. However, it would be a serious mistake to identify the common material substratum with the nucleus and the differentiating principle with the electrons, for both nucleus and electrons are material elements and hylomorphically composed.

The fact that chemical compounds continue to have the typical X-ray spectra of their component elements does not militate against the unity of the substantial form in such compounds. First, because it is doubtful whether the compound remains intact under X-ray treatment; secondly, because the permanence of the X-ray spectrum can be explained by the virtual (not actual) presence of the elements, i.e., the elements contribute some of their qualities to the compound.

The impurity of bodies larger than a molecule does not necessarily mean that such bodies have more than one substantial form. It can be explained by admitting that the form of such a body defies classification into idealized physical or philosophical systems, for there is no reason why a single form in different parts of matter could not give rise to different characteristics. The whole universe cannot be considered as a single substance, because man's experience tells him that he is not just a part of a larger whole but a distinct being. Below man, other individual substances can be distinguished if we keep in mind that the very notion of individual substance diminishes in value on the non-human level and needs to retain only a minimum of spatio-temporal natural cohesion to justify its usage with respect to the non-living world. This kind of cohesion may be considered to exist in each molecule of gases and liquids, isolated molecules of solids, crystals, and larger units resulting from an inherent pattern of organization. It is lacking in a mere heap of sand. On the other hand, it is practically impossible to determine whether one has to do with a substantially unified individual or a mere aggregate in the case of the many intermediary ways in which material objects can be united.

SUGGESTED READINGS

60. Henry J. Koren, *Readings in the Philosophy of Nature:*

Erwin Schrödinger, *What is an Elementary Particle?*, pp. 340 ff.

Andrew G. van Melsen, *What are the Individual Substances in Matter?*, pp. 352 ff.

Joseph Bobik, *St. Thomas on the Individuation of Bodily Substances*, pp. 327 ff.[12]

Peter Hoenen, *The Virtual Presence of Elemental Forms in the Compound*, pp. 191 ff.

---

[12]The metaphysical basis of individuation has not been considered in this chapter, because we have treated in it our *Introduction to Metaphysics*, ch. V.

An Introduction to the Philosophy of Nature

Andrew G. van Melsen, *From Atoms to Atom,* Pittsburgh, 1952, ch. V, pp. 167 ff. Modern atomic theory.

Louis de Broglie, *Matter and Light, New York,* n.d., pp. 217 ff. Continuity and individuality in modern physics.

CHAPTER FIVE

DYNAMISM, MECHANISM, AND HYLOSYSTEMISM

1. DYNAMISM

The Theory

61. The principal exponent, if not the founder, of dynamism was the eighteenth century Jesuit Boscovich.[1] Slightly different dynamistic theories were proposed by Leibniz, Kant,[2] Carbonelle, Palmieri, and Hirn.[3] The the various systems have the following salient characteristics:

1. Everything material is composed of unextended points or elements.

2. These elements are nothing but centers of active forces of attraction and repulsion.

3. The forces act at a distance (this point is denied by Leibniz and Palmieri).

By means of these forces, the dynamists claim, the material world can be satisfactorily explained.

This brief statement of dynamism will have to suffice for our purpose.

Critique

62. *Dynamism Cannot Explain Extension.* One of the most striking characteristics of the world as it reveals itself to us is its extension in space: different parts of it

---

[1] *Theoria philosophiae naturalis,* Venice, 1763 (first edition, 1758).
[2] *Monadologia physica,* 1756; *Metaphysische Anfangsgruende der Naturwissenschaft,* 1786.
[3] Cf. D. Nys, *Cosmology,* vol. I, Milwaukee, 1942, pp. 225 ff.

occupy different positions separated by a distance. But if everything material is composed only of unextended points, as the dynamists claim, extension can never arise. No matter how many unextended points are "joined" together, they do not constitute an extended whole. Having no parts, they cannot merely touch one another but of necessity must coincide entirely.

If, with Boscowich, one claims that the points remain at a distance from one another and thus constitute and extended body by means of their relationships of mutual distances, extension is surreptitiously introduced. For distance is essentially connected with the idea of joining two points by means of a line, and any line is necessarily extended and therefore cannot be constituted by unextended points.

This difficulty is not removed by claiming that a point generates extension by its motion. Actual motion presupposes the possibility of motion. But to be possible, motion needs a place in which it can occur, i.e., extension. Accordingly, we may conclude that unextended points cannot give rise to the extension which characterizes all material reality. Therefore, the first principle of dynamism is unsatisfactory.

63. *Matter is Not Purely Active.* The second principle of dynamism (all material elements are purely active) cannot be accepted. An element which is totally active either acts on others or solely on itself. If it acts on others, these others are acted upon and therefore passive in this respect. If it acts only on itself, this action cannot give rise to any changes in the others; therefore, such an action cannot explain why any change should result in the relationship which the various active elements have to one another.

Moreover, the exclusion of passivity in matter flatly contradicts experience. The world, as it reveals itself to us, is neither totally active nor wholly passive, but a constant interplay of acting and being acted upon, of activity and passivity.

64. *Material Forces Do Not Act at a Distance.* Such an action seems to be metaphysically *impossible*. To be acted upon by an agent, the material recipient must be in local contact with the agent. For a material agent can act only upon a recipient which is capable of being acted upon here and now. But a necessary condition for this capacity is that both agent and recipient belong to the same material system, and this requires that there be either immediate or mediate local contact. Otherwise the action emanating from the material agent, in passing to the recipient, would have to traverse a vacuum and exist there autonomously without a substantial support.[4]

Moreover, all available evidence indicates that action at a distance *de facto* does not occur in nature. The intensity of any material action always decreases with the distance separating the agent from the recipient. This fact indicates that there must be an intermediary element by which the action of the agent is transmitted to the recipient.

2. MECHANISM

65. *The Theory.* Mechanism is a venerable old theory whose first beginnings go back to the dawn of philosophy in Greece. Democritus (c. 460-370 B. C.) and Epicurus (342-270 B. C.) may be considered its most prominent representatives in ancient times. Democritus tried to solve the problem of change[5] by claiming that the world consists of qualitatively undifferentiated indivisible particles ("atoms") whose local motion renders all changes intelligible. Descartes[6] (1596-1650) gave a new impetus to

---

[4]Concerning the necessity of a substantial support for action, cf. the author's *Metaphysics*, nos. 182 ff.
[5]Concerning this problem, cf. *op. cit.*, nos. 114 ff.
[6]*Principia philosophiae, Amsterdam*, 1644.

mechanism. He claimed that the universe is composed of infinitely divisible homogeneous matter, devoid of any intrinsic principle of activity, but subject to the local motion imparted to it by the Creator. This local motion alone suffices to explain all changes in the universe. To say it briefly, there is nothing but matter in motion. Accordingly, nature can be explained adequately in terms of mechanical models.

Following Descartes, mechanism became the system accepted by almost all men of research. It continued in this privileged position until the end of the nineteenth century when its grip on science was broken by the development of the critique of the sciences. No longer is the claim made that models alone give us a definite insight into the nature of material reality. Nevertheless, the mechanical view continues to exercise a powerful attraction and somehow the hope persists that local motion of particles alone will ultimately render any other explanations of the material world entirely superfluous.

66. *Critique.* Two aspects of mechanism should be clearly distinguished—namely, its value as a scientific theory and its ability to solve philosophical problems of matter. The first of these two lies beyond the scope of this study and evidently has to be left to the critique of competent scientists. The second definitely pertains to the philosopher. It is concerned with the question whether or not mechanism provides an adequate explanation for the philosophical problems which it claims to solve or render superfluous.

Philosophically speaking, Democritus' mechanism was a dismal attempt to solve Parmenides' dilemma of being and change. As we have seen in metaphysics,[7] Parmenides rejected the possibility of change because the statement "change exists" is not intelligible but a contradiction in

---

[7]Cf. the author's *Metaphysics,* no. 115.

terms.[8] Thus it would be similar to a square circle. Democritus tried to circumvent the dilemma by claiming that it is not so difficult to understand tiny changes in position and on this basis proceeded to explain the phenomena of matter. Evidently, this philosophical "solution" did not dispose of the problem of change, for if change, like a square circle, is unintelligible, a tiny change in position is just as unintelligible as a little square circle. Accordingly, although there is an answer to Parmenides' dilemma,[9] Democritus' mechanism failed to supply it. Therefore it is philosophically not acceptable.

A similar answer must be given with respect to Cartesian mechanism and modern mechanistic aspirations. Let us suppose that all changes in matter could be reduced to a shift in position of material elements. As a physical theory, mechanism would then have been completely successful. Nevertheless, it would not have solved the philosophical problem of change. The reason is that such a successful physical theory simply reduces a multitude of different kinds of changes to one type, but does not even raise the question as to why material change is possible at all i.e., under what conditions it *can be* and does not constitute an internal contradiction. Again, mechanism does not even attempt to reply to the question why different material objects can have the same fundamental characteristics and thereby show themselves endowed with the *same* nature. Yet it is precisely such questions which pertain to the philosophy of nature. For this reason we may say that mechanism cannot be proposed as a theory which solves *all* problems of matter,

---

[8]Change or coming-to-be would mean either that being comes to be being or that non-being comes to be being. But being cannot come to be, for it already is; non-being cannot come to be, for from nothing nothing can come. Cf. *ibidem.*

[9]It is supplied by Aristotle's distinction of being into being-in-act and being-in-potency. Change means a transition from being-in-potency to being-in-act, hence it is encompassed by being and, consequently, intelligible. Cf. *ibidem.*

for it simply takes for granted the solution of some of these problems—the philosophical ones. Philosophically, therefore, it is unsatisfactory.

*3. HYLOSYSTEMISM

67. The Theory. Impressed by the striking success of modern physical science, A. Mitterer[10] in Germany and Celestine Bittle[11] in the United States attempted to construct a philosophical theory on the basis of the data of science. It is called hylosystemism. According to this theory an inorganic body is an atomic energy system composed of subatomic particles which are united into a dynamic system that works as a functional unit. This is all that can be said about the essence of a body. Hylosystemists explicitly reject the matter-form composition of traditional philosophy as an antiquated view, because their attempts to use it in explaining the modern data of science were not successful.

68. Critique. Our criticism of this theory can be very brief.[12] Leaving its scientific value to the judgment of competent physicists, we may point out that, despite its claim to be philosophical, hylosystemism does not reply to any of the strictly philosophical questions regarding matter. All it does is repeat or rearrange the statements of science without even considering the conditions under which material change is intelligible or bodies can possess the same nature. Therefore, it is philosophically inadequate.

Of course, it is true that, as the hylosystemists say, the matter-form theory of traditional philosophy fails to ex-

---

[10]*Wandel des Weltbild von Thomas auf Heute,* vol. I, Innsbrück, 1935; vol. II, Bresasone, 1936.

[11]*From Aether to Cosmos,* Milwaukee, 1941, pp. 324 ff.

[12]For a more detailed critique, see Br. Benignus Gerrity, *Nature Knowledge and God,* Milwaukee, 1949, pp. 136 ff.; H. M. Braun, "Hylosystemismus oder Hylemorphismus?" *Divus Thomas* (Fr.), 1938, vol. 16, pp. 420-458.

plain the modern data of science. However, they should
have kept in mind that the purpose of the philosophy of
nature is not to provide a specific explanation of such
phenomena, but merely to account for the most fundamental characteristics of all material being and that with
respect to these characteristics the physical explanation of
corporeal composition is wholly irrelevant.

SUMMARY

69. Dynamism claims that the ultimate units of matter
are unextended elements, endowed only with the active
forces of attraction and repulsion which act at a distance.
This theory is unsatisfactory, because:

1. Unextended points can never give rise to extended
   bodies.

2. Matter that is purely active cannot explain why the
   action of a body should modify anything in surrounding bodies.

3. Action at a distance would have to exist in a vacuum
   without a substantial support.

Mechanism endeavors to explain the world solely in
terms of matter in motion, so that mechanical models would
make any other explanation superfluous. Philosophically,
it is not satisfactory, for it simply takes for granted that
motion can exist.

*Hylosystemism makes the philosophical essence of mat-
ter consist in an atomic energy system of subatomic particles united into a functionally unified dynamic whole.
This theory confuses science with philosophy and fails to
account for the most fundamental aspects of material being.

SUGGESTED READINGS

70. Henry J. Koren, *Readings in the Philosophy of Nature:*

a. DYNAMISM

R. J. Boscovich, *Theory of the Philosophy of Nature,* pp. 102 ff.

Immanuel Kant, *Physical Monadology,* pp. 105 f. *Metaphysical Foundations of Physical Science,* pp. 106 ff.

Fernard Renoirte, *Critique of Dynamism,* pp. 108 ff.

b. MECHANISM

Rene Descartes, *Philosophical Principles of Nature,* pp. 111 ff.

Fernand Renoirte, *Critique of Mechanism,* pp. 115 ff.

c. HYLOSYSTEMISM

Celestine Bittle, *The Hylomeric Constitution of Bodies,* pp. 120 f.

Benignus Gerrity, *Examination of Hylosystemism,* pp. 127 ff.

P. Henry van Laer, *Philosophico-Scientific Problems,* Pittsburgh, 1953, ch. III (action at a distance).

Andrew G. van Melsen, *From Atomos to Atom,* Pittsburgh, 1952, (mechanism).

Désiré Nys, *Cosmology,* Milwaukee, 1942, vol. I (mechanism and dynamism).

SECTION TWO

THE PROPERTIES OF MATTER

In this section we will consider the general characteristics of material beings. The first and most striking of these features undoubtedly is extension or quantity, to which we will devote Chapter Six. Next we will consider motion (Chapter VII), place, space and time (Chapters VIII, IX and X). Material qualities will occupy our attention in Chapter XI. The final chapter (XII) will be devoted to a consideration of causality in material beings.

CHAPTER SIX

QUANTITY

71. Quantity or extension cannot be properly defined because it is one of the primordial concepts which man derives from experience. It is often described as the status of "having parts outside parts." Although this description may be useful, it is not very good, for it introduces the notions of "part" and "outside," which presuppose extension. The idea of extension arises from the observation that a body can be divided inasmuch as we grasp immediately that such a possibility is not founded on the body's color, heat, softness or any other such quality, but solely on a property which we indicate by the term "extension."

Regarding quantity, the following philosophical problems will be considered. First of all, we will ask whether quantity is to be identified with bodily being or really distinct from it. Secondly, we will investigate the nature of the continuum. The last question is whether extension may be said to characterize all matter.[1]

1. QUANTITY AND MATERIAL SUBSTANCE

72. The real distinction of quantity from the material substance whose quantity it is follows from the considerations of substance in metaphysics.[2] We may briefly propose the proof as follows:

---

[1] We omit the question which one among the many formal effects attributed to quantity (divisibility, measurability, impenetrability, aptitudinal local extension, actual local extension, plurality of parts, order of parts among themselves) is primary and therefore can never be absent in a quantified body. The answer is of importance only for the theology of the Holy Eucharist and therefore may be omitted in this general college text. For a brief survey of the various views, cf. John O'Neill, *Cosmology*, London, 1923, pp. 186-191.

[2] Cf. the author's *Metaphysics*, ch. 8.

If quantity and material substance were really identical, one could not change without the other. This should be clear from the very meaning of real identity. But a material substance or body may undergo changes in quantity, e.g., growth, while it remains the same body, as is clear from experience. Thus it follows that quantity and body are really distinct.

Moreover, material beings belonging to the same species are only individually distinct. Nevertheless, they may have specifically different quantities; e. g., two cows whose weights are 350 and 400 lbs. This specific substantial identity, coupled with the specific difference in quantity, indicates that quantity cannot be identified with the essence of a material substance, but is something added to the essence.

On the other hand, quantity is not something which can exist autonomously. If it exists in reality, it will always exist as a mode of being of a real subject. Although it is possible, for instance, to understand what is meant by "five foot long" without considering the subject whose length it is, the length itself cannot exist except insofar as there exists something which is five foot long. For this reason we say that quantity is an accident of a material substance, taking the term "accident" as opposed to "substance" and, therefore, expressing that quantity depends on a subject for its existence.

2. THE CONTINUUM

73. Quantity is usually divided into *discrete* quantity or number and *continuous* quantity. Continuity should be distinguished from mere contiguity. In contiguity the extremes of two extended bodies are in contact but they are not the same. When there is question of continuity, however, we are not dealing with two bodies but with one and the same extended being.

A continuum may be either *successive* or *permanent*. The first is exemplified by motion and time. The permanent continuum can be either *mathematical* or *physical*. Examples of mathematical continua are the line (one-dimensional), the surface (two-dimensional), and the solid (three-dimensional). The physical continuum is the same as an essentially unified extended body, e.g., a plant or an animal. We will consider here the permanent continuum and reserve the study of the successive continuum for later chapters.

74. *The Continuum Does Not Have Actual Parts, but Only Potential Parts.* By "parts" we mean here integral extended portions, such as halves or thirds. Such parts would exist actually only if they had a "to be" of their own. But a continuum is an essentially unified whole and not a mere juxtaposition of separate parts, and therefore is actually one. Now it is impossible that what is actually one being be also actually many beings. For this reason it appears to be a metaphysical contradiction for the parts of the continuum to be *actual*.

By excluding the actuality of extended parts in a continuum we do not at all deny that mentally we are able to distinguish parts or that a continuum may be physically divided into actual parts, but merely want to assert that such parts do not actually exist prior to the act of division. As a matter of fact, hardly anyone would deny the divisibility of the continuum. Expressed in metaphysical language, this divisibility means that the continuum has *potential* parts.

We may even go further and claim that these parts exists in immediate potency for actuation, for all that is required to make them actual is the division of the whole. An illustration of the point may be taken from plants: a part can be severed from the whole in such a way that it continues to exist as a plant. Prior to the severance, this part was in immediate potency to separate existence as an essentially unified being, and the sole act of division made the part pass from potential existence to actual existence.[3]

*The *objection* could be raised that the parts of a continuum, e.g., the roots and leaves of a plant, act. Therefore, since action follows being, these parts must also actually exist. (This argument, however, would be valid only if it were demonstrated that the actions belong to each part as to the ultimate principle which acts (the supposit) and not to the whole as acting through its parts.)

75. _The Continuum Remains Infinitely Divisible into Extended Parts._ In making this claim we pay attention only to the nature of the continuum as such and abstract from limitations that may be imposed on its divisibility from other viewpoints, such as the requirements of its specific physical nature. If an extended reality is divided below a certain minimum, say, an atom, its specific nature may not be capable of existing any longer in the resulting parts, so that in this sense a body of such a specific nature does not remain infinitely divisible. In other words, the expression: the continuum infinitely remains divisible, is equivalent to the assertion that the continuum does not consists of unextended parts, it cannot be resolved into unextended points.

The *proof* is as follows:

The addition of the unextended to the unextended can never result in the extended, for otherwise non-being would give rise to being. Therefore, the extended cannot consist of unextended parts, but must have extended parts. Now any extended part itself can be divided again for the same reason as the original extended whole. And these new parts also must be extended. And so on to infinity.

---

[3]Cf. the author's *Animate Nature,* no. 58.

76. The *objection*[4] could be raised that this divisibility would imply an infinite number of parts, which is impossible. While we are willing to admit that an infinite number of *actual* parts is not possible, it should be remembered that the parts of a continuum are not actual but merely potential. Therefore, no actual infinite number will result.

If one insists that it is of the very essence of a potency to be capable of actuation, and therefore that an actually infinite number could result, the objection overlooks a vital point—namely, that it is in principle impossible to actuate all these potencies simultaneously. Yet this simultaneous actuation would have to be possible before there would be a contradiction. The reason why the simultaneous actuation cannot take place is the following. Any act of division of a continuum will necessarily result in extended parts which remain divisible, and this divisibility can be actuated only by a new act of dividing into extended parts. Consequently, no matter how powerful an agent be, its action can never in a single stroke actuate all the potential parts. Therefore, the actuation will necessarily have a successive character and thus does not imply an actually infinite number.

Another difficulty arises from a so-called thought experiment. Let us assume that a perfect sphere stands in top of a perfect plane. These two have only one point in which they touch. But by rolling over the plane the sphere would produce an extended line. Consequently, the extended consists of unextended points and not of extended parts. This objection, however, fails to take into consideration that, in addition to the unextended point of contact, it introduces the extension of continuous motion. It is precisely the successive continuum of motion which gives rise to the continuous line.[5]

---

[4]Cf. P. Hoenen, *Cosmologia,* nos. 18 ff.
[5]Motion itself presupposes an extended whole in which it can take place.

3. MATTER IS CHARACTERIZED BY EXTENSION[6]

77. In recent times occasionally the claim is made that science has discovered certain kinds of material phenomena which are not characterized by extension so that extension can no longer be considered as a property, in the strict sense of the term, of matter.

"Ordinary" Matter. Scarcely anyone would question the extended character of what we may call "ordinary" matter. The danger here lies rather in the opposite extreme—namely, the identification of extension with the very essence of matter, as was claimed by Descartes and his followers.

Fields of Forces. There is more opportunity for divergence of views with respect to radiation quanta and electromagnetic and gravitational fields.[7] To begin with the latter, everyone is ready to admit that their mathematical description involves extension, but it is sometimes denied that these fields have real extension. However, if the mathematical descriptions indicate real spatially dispersed properties, then the spatially dispersed character of these properties demands a spatially extended substratum. Whatever one may think about the nature of this substratum, it should be clear that these fields are extended.

Radiation quanta result from the meeting of positive and negative electrons. Although their spatial structure or extension is not directly open to observation, nevertheless they are of an extended nature. The reason is that they exhibit properties which of necessity imply extension. For instance, they are localized through contact with "or-

---

[6]Cf. P. Henry van Laer, *Philosophico-Scientific Problems,* Pittsburgh, 1953, Ch. 2, pp. 14-27.

[7]A radiation quantum is the unit of energy emitted in the meeting of a positive and a negative electron. The "fields" referred to in the text are the areas surrounding an electromagnetic body or a body having a heavy mass in which the forces of electromagnetism and gravitation work.

dinary" matter, the direction of their motion can be described in terms of extended matter, they can collide and transfer their energy and momentum. All these phenomena indicate that radiation quanta are of an extended nature.

Why Extension Is Denied. The reason why the extended and even the material nature of these physical phenomena is sometimes denied may perhaps be sought in the unconscious identification of matter with mass. The concept of mass, as determined by the weight of a body at rest,[8] does not apply to the phenomena of radiation because they are not at rest, and it is meaningless with respect to gravitational and electromagnetic fields. Hence for one who identifies matter with mass, the above-indicated phenomena would be immaterial. But, as was pointed out in the preceding chapter, such an identification is not permissible.

We may, therefore, conclude that extension or quantity is something that always accompanies material beings as they are known from experience. On the other hand, nonmaterial beings or spirits do not possess extension, for they are simple and thus do not have any "parts outside parts" which could be affected by quantity. Thus it follows that extension is a characteristic or criterion of matter.

*HISTORICAL NOTES

78. Berkeley (1685-1753) and other idealists denied the reality of extension. For *Kant,* extension is merely the *a priori* form according to which our mind perceives the phenomena of the material world.

As was mentioned, *Descartes* identified extension with the very essence of material being.

---

[8]The mass in question is so-called "rest" mass. "Heavy" mass is mass causing a gravitational field; "inertial" mass is the measure of resistance to acceleration. The two are equal, and when at rest they are called "rest mass."

Boscovich denied the reality of the continuum, but admitted that spatially distant points could be perceived as if there were a continuum.

Some seventeenth century philosophers (e.g., *Arriega* and *Oviedo*) and perhaps also the ancient Pythagorians admitted that the continuum consisted of indivisible parts. Others such as *John of St. Thomas* (1589-1644) and *Joseph Gredt* (1863-1940) claimed that it has a plurality of actual parts. Not understanding the distinction between actual and potential real parts, but realizing the infinite divisibility of the continuum, *Charles Renouvier* (1815-1903) was driven to deny the reality of the continuum.

SUMMARY

79. Quantity, which is usually described as having "parts outside parts," is what makes a body extended. Extension is not really identical with the substance whose extension it is, for a change in one does not necessarily imply a change in the other. Quantity or extension is to be conceived as a real accident of material being, in the sense that it does not exist separately but is a mode of being proper to a body.

The continuum or essentially unified extended body has no actual parts, i.e., parts existing through a "to be" of their own, for otherwise the continuum itself would not be essentially one but merely an aggregate. The continuum, however, has potential parts, i.e., parts than can be made actual through division.

A continuum, taken as such, is infinitely divisible into extended parts. The reason is that otherwise the continuum would ultimately consists of unextended parts, which is impossible because the unextended cannot give rise to the extended. Note, however, that there is question here only of infinite divisibility and not of an infinite number of actual parts arising from division and existing simultaneously. Only successive actuation of potential parts is possible, so that there will never result an infinite number of actual parts.

Extension is a fundamental characteristic or property of matter and always accompanies material beings as we know them from experience.

SUGGESTED READINGS

80. Aristotle, *Physica,* bk. V, ch. 3 VI, ch. 3; *Metaphysica,* bk. VII, ch. 13.

Thomas Aquinas, *In XI Metaphysic,* lect. 13 no. 2414; in *VI Physic.,* lect. 1; in *IV Sentent.* d. 12, q. 1., a. 1, sol. 3.

Henry J. Koren, *Readings in the Philosophy of Nature:*

John O'Neill, *The Essence of Quantity,* pp. 207 ff.

Vincent E. Smith, *The Continuum,* pp. 212 ff.

P. Henry van Laer, *Extension as the Criterion of Matter,* pp. 216 ff.

Andrew G. van Melsen, *The Philosophy of Nature,* ch. V, sect. 1.

CHAPTER SEVEN

MOTION

81. Any transition from one state of being to another or any change may be called motion in a broad sense of the term. In this way the term applies also to substantial change and other modifications which take place instantaneously At present, however, we want to take motion in its proper sense as continuous motion, i.e., a change in which the transition from one state of being to another take place by passing successively and uninterruptedly through intermediary stages. Such motions appear to occur in quantity (increase and decrease), quality (alteration), or place (locomotion or motion in its narrowest sense).

1. ANALYSIS OF MOTION

From immediate experience everyone knows in a confused way what motion is. However, it is not so easy to determine what kind of a being motion is.

Let us attempt to analyze motion in an example and see if we can arrive at a satisfactory description. For this purpose we may take the flight of a bullet fired at a target. Before being fired, the bullet does not yet move but it is merely in potency to motion. Once it has reached the target, it no longer moves to the target: its motion has reached its end and is no longer because the bullet is fully "in act" with respect to the object of the motion. In other words, motion does not actually exist in either the starting point or the terminus of the motion. Accordingly, if there is any motion, it will be in between the starting point (S) and the terminus (T), so that motion will be something between "in potency" and "in act."

In a mechanical model the trajectory may be represented by a line and the bullet by a point moving along the line. However, care must be taken not to conceive the bullet as moving *in* any point between S and T, for motion in an unextended point is not possible. Motion occurs precisely in between any two points, in an extended part of the trajectory, insofar as the bullet *passes* in a continuous way *through* one point after the other. Of course, we may mentally consider the bullet at any given point between S and T and say of it: when it passes through this point, it is in motion. Let us call this point X.

If the bullet moves in passing through X, it *was moving* in the past prior to reaching X, for any part of a continuum is infinitely divisible, so that there are always intermediary points between X and S. It will be true also that the bullet *will be moving* in the future because of the continuous nature of the interval between X and T. If the bullet had not yet moved before reaching X, it would not be moving through X but merely have its starting point in X. If it would no longer move after reaching X, it would not be moving through X, but X would be the terminus of its motion.

Thus motion appears to possess something of the character of potency and something of the character of act. On the one hand, it implies the past actuation of a potency to motion but, on the other, it contains also a still unactuated potency to further motion. Motion, therefore, is the act of a being which was in potency to motion and still is in potency to further motion. For this reason motion is aptly described as *"the act of a being in potency insofar as it still is in potency."*[1]

82. *Motion as an Imperfect Act.* The potential character implied by motion shows that motion is not a perfect

---

[1]Aristotle, *Physica,* bk. III, ch. 1, 201a 10.

but an imperfect act. Not every imperfect act, however, is motion. We may say, for instance, that water with a temperature of 60° has the act of heat "imperfectly" in the sense that water can have a higher degree of heat. While having the less intense act of heat, the water is also in potency to more heat but, unless it is actually being heated, it is not moving toward a more intense act of heat. Thus the imperfect character of motion does not consist in the fact that there is an imperfect act coupled with a potency for more motion, but in this that the actuality of motion itself in its very nature implies an order of further progress in the actualization of its potency.

Irreducibility of Motion. Accordingly, motion is a dynamic perfection. It can exist only in a fluid, continuous, or progressive state but never in a static condition. For this reason it is impossible to reduce motion to any kind of static act or perfection. Every attempt to describe or explain it in terms of static entities destroys its very nature. At most, such an attempt will succeed in describing something to which or from which there was or will be motion (the terminus or principle of motion), but not motion itself.

2. The Reality of Motion

83. In the preceding pages we stressed the fluid nature of motion and said that any *actually* moving object *was* moving in the past and *will be moving* in the future. The past, however, no longer exists, and the future is not yet. But past and future motion are separated only by an indivisible point in which the object does not move.[2] Therefore, motion does not exist. Or to say it differently and briefly, what is composed of non-existing parts does not

---

[2] If the object moved in a point, the unextended point would contain the extended continuum of motion.

exist But the parts of motion do not exist. Therefore motion does not exist.

The solution of this difficulty against the reality of motion is as follows. We may conclude to the non-existence of a whole whose parts do not exist if the whole in question is supposed to be composed of *actual* parts. However, a continuum does not have any actual parts, but only potential parts. In other words, neither the past nor the future phases of motion actually exist as such, but the only reality is the motion itself taken in its totality.

We may *mentally* divide this totality into past and future "parts," but this mental division does not result in a real interruption of the single continuous fluid reality of motion. If, on the other hand, we *really* interrupt the motion at any point of its course, thereby making its past and future parts actually distinct, then it is true that motion no longer exist. In that case the point of interruption has become the new starting point of possible future motion.[3]

84. *Zeno's Arguments Against Motion.* Zeno of Elea and his followers formulated other famous dialectical arguments against motion (and even any kind of change). First of all, they argued, in moving from S to T the object would have to pass through an infinite number of intermediary points, which is impossible.

Secondly, if motion were real, a fast runner like Achilles could never overtake a slow-moving tortoise which is given a small handicap. For when he reaches the point where the tortoise started, this animal will have advanced a short distance, so that Achilles will have to travel also this distance before he can overtake the tortoise. And so on to infinity. Hence Achilles would come constantly closer but never be able to catch up with the tortoise.

---

[3]Cf. P. Hoenen, *Cosmologia*, no. 157.

Thirdly, at every moment of time the arrow shot from a bow does not move. Consequently, it does not move in the whole of time.[4]

All these difficulties are based on misunderstandings of the true nature proper to the continuum. With respect to the first, although points can be distinguished to infinity between the start and the end of a continuum, the continuum does not consist of unextended points but is a single extended whole. Neither does motion consist in a series of discontinuous actions but it is a single continuous whole. The second difficulty assumes that the continuum contains an infinite number of actual parts, which was rejected in the preceding chapter (no. 74). The last argument, likewise, takes for granted that the continuous flow of time is made up of indivisible moments, which is against the continuity of time.

3. The Unity of Motion

85. The question may be raised as to what justifies us in conceiving a motion, despite its dispersion in time, as a single unified whole.

It would not be sufficient to seek this justification in the fact that one and the same being perdures as the identical subject of the motion. For the same subject may successfully receive individually distinct determinations of its potentiality. Neither would it suffice to appeal to the unity of the efficient cause producing the motion, for several distinct causes may, and usually do, concur in the production of a concrete motion.

The only justification for the asserted unity of motion lies in final causality. From the very start the moving object tends to a certain end, and this tendency perdures throughout the whole motion and determines its direction.

---

[4]Cf. Aristotle, *Physica*, bk. VI, ch. 9 and bk. VIII, ch. 8. We omit the fourth argument of the Eleatics because it is rather involved and appears to be based on an obviously false assumption.

In every phase of the motion, the directional tendency of the subsequent phase is potentially present in the actual tendency of the motion. Since this tendency does not change as long as the motion continues, it gives unity to the motion in question.

It is to be noted that this tendency results from the combined influence of all the causes acting upon the object at the moment it begins to move. Each of these causes in acting has its own finality and the combination of the finalities inherent in these actions gives rise to the finality or tendency proper to the object as it begins to move here and now. Evidently, the inherent finality of the moving object may differ from the purpose assigned to its motion by a human mover who does not fully control all the forces that are at work. The important point here, however, is not that this extrinsic purpose be reached, but that throughout the motion the same inherent final tendency, as resulting from the combination of all moving factors, remains present.

4. Motion and the Law of Inertia

86. According to the law of inertia, a body at rest does not begin to move unless acted upon by an external agent, but once set in motion, it continues uniformly in the same straight line unless acted upon by an external force.[5] At first sight, this law seems to imply that no efficient cause is needed for the continued uniform motion of a body, but only for the acceleration or deceleration of that motion. As a matter of fact, it is in this sense that the law of inertia is often interpreted and made to support the

---

[5] It is interesting to note that Aristotle, while rejecting the void, formulated a statement resembling the principle of inertia: "No one could say why a thing once set in motion should stop anywhere, for why should it stop *here* rather than *there?* So that a thing will either be at rest or must be moved *ad infinitum,* unless something more powerful get in its way." *Physica,* bk. IV, ch. 8, 215a 19.

claim that Aristotelian metaphysics contradicts the laws of physics.

Such an interpretation, however, would imply a metaphysical absurdity, for it would mean that a real effect (a change of place) would come about without a cause.[6] On the other hand, it is equally unjustifiable to reject the law of inertia as being against "sound" reason. As usually happens when science appears to contradict philosophy, there is here an ambiguity of terms. When scientists deny that there is any need for a physical force to explain inertial motion, they mean that, once the body is set into motion, there is no need for an external agent to keep acting on this body to make it move. When philosophy, on the other hand, asserts that inertial motion needs an efficient cause, it does not mean that the external agent has to continue the actual exercise of its causality, but only that the motion in question is not self-explanatory, i.e., it finds its explanation in a quality imparted to the moving body by the external agent and will continue as long as this quality is present in the body. This quality, then, is the cause producing the uniform motion. It is usually indicated by the term "impetus."

From the preceding considerations it follows, therefore, that the inertial motion of bodies does not prove anything against the metaphysical principle of causality: "whatever is in motion is moved by another."

*HISTORICAL NOTES

87. The existence of motion was denied by *Zeno* (c. 490-c. 430 B. C.) and the Eleatics. The idealists consider motion as a phenomenon of consciousness.

Descartes ridiculed *Aristotle's* definition of motion, quoted in this chapter, as unintelligible "hocus-pocus" serving only to obscure what everybody understands im-

---

6 Cf. ch. XII.

mediately.[7] He himself, however, did not understand it sufficiently to offer an adequate solution of Zeno's objections.[8]

One reason why, starting from the seventeenth century, Aristotle's philosophy of motion encountered so much opposition and even became an important factor in the total rejection of his teachings, was that his metaphysical analysis was thoroughly mixed with antiquated physical views. The notions of "natural place" and "natural motion" seemed to play too great a role in it. Nevertheless, his analysis can be divested of these physical encumbrances, as we have done in the preceding pages, and then presents itself as a metaphysically sound explanation of motion.

As to the cause of continuous motion, there is fairly general agreement in calling it impetus, but opinions differ about the further determination of its nature.

SUMMARY

88. Motion is not possible in an unextended point but only in a continuum. If a body is in motion when passing a certain point, it was moving in the past and will be moving in the future. Motion, therefore, is the act of a being which was in potency to motion and remains in potency to motion. The future actuation of this potentiality for motion is implied in the very actuality of the present motion. It is, therefore, defined as the act of a being in potency insofar as it is in potency. Thus motion is a continuous or fluid perfection and cannot be reduced to a static condition.

Although the past and future parts of a motion do not exist in the present, and the present is an indivisible point in which there can be no motion, it does not follow that motion is not real. A whole whose parts are non-existent

---

[7]*Rules for the Direction of the Mind,* Rule XII (Dover edition of *Philosophical Works of Descartes,* vol. I, p. 46).

[8]*Correspondence,* Adam et Tannery ed., vol. IV, p. 445. Cf. Hoenen, *Cosmologia,* no. 159 d.

does not exist if it is supposed to consist of actual parts. But motion is a continuum and therefore its parts are not actual but only potential. To make them actual, we would have to really interrupt the motion and then, of course, the motion would no longer exist. But as long as we merely mentally distinguish the parts, the continuity of motion is not broken and therefore the motion can continue to exist.

Keeping in mind that the extended continuum does not consist of an infinity of unextended points or of extended actual parts, we should have no difficulty in solving Zeno's main arguments against the possibility of motion.

Despite its temporal dispersion in the past and the future, motion is a single unified whole. The reason does not lie in the unity of the subject that is moved, nor in that of the cause producing the beginning of the motion, but in the inherent final causality or tendency of the motion. For in every phase of the motion the actual tendency potentially contains the tendency of the subsequent phase, and this tendency does not change as long as the motion continues without being subjected to forces giving rise to modifications of this tendency, i.e., causing a new motion.

The law of inertia does not violate the principle of efficient causality, but merely denies the need for the continued exercise of a physical force by an external agent outside the moving body. Hence this law cannot be adduced against the principle that whatever is in motion is moved by another.

SUGGESTED READINGS

89. Aristotle, *Physica,* bk. III, chs. 1-3.

Thomas Aquinas, *Comment. in III Physic.,* lect. 1-5.

Henry J. Koren, *Readings in the Philosophy of Nature:* Aristotle, *The Nature of Motion,* pp. 232 ff.

An Introduction to the Philosophy of Nature

Andrew G. van Melsen, *Modern Physics and Aristotle's Analysis of Motion,* pp. 237 ff.

Aristotle, *Zeno's Arguments for the Impossibility of Motion,* pp. 240 ff.

P. Hoenen, *Cosmologia,* nos. 143-162 and Notae VIII and IX.

Gavin Ardley, "The Physics of Local Motion," *The Thomist,* 1954, pp. 145-185. A plea for a return to Aristotelian physics with respect to the causality of motion.

CHAPTER EIGHT

PLACE

1. THE NATURE AND REALITY OF PLACE

90. *Nature of Place.* When we speak of place we mean the position a material object occupies in reference to other objects. For instance, we say that the book is on the table or the cat in the garden. Other objects may occupy the same places indicated in these examples; hence we have to distinguish common and proper place. By the *proper* place of an object we mean the place pertaining to this object and not to anything else. Such a place is determined by the immediate surroundings of the object and therefore may be described as the innermost boundary of what surrounds the object in question.

However, this description is not yet sufficient. If, for example, I fill a glass with water, the inner surface of the glass may be considered the boundary of the water. But if the glass of water is transferred from the kitchen to the dining-room, we do not say that the water is still in the same place. In other words, by place we mean the immediate immobile surroundings of a body. Thus we arrive at Aristotle's definition of place as the "innermost immobile boundary of what immediately surrounds an object."

The immobility of the surrounding matter, however, should be understood only in a formal sense. For instance, if a rock is located in the middle of a stream, the surrounding water is not motionless with respect to the rock. It is sufficient that the surface of the water touching the rock remains the same with respect to some

---

[1]*Physica,* bk. IV, ch. 4, 212a 10.

motionless point of reference. Materially, the surrounding water moves, but its shape around the rock remains the same same. The surface, then, is to be taken insofar as it indicates a definite position in the world.

91. *Relativity of Place.* A further difficulty remains even if we take these surroundings formally. One can legitimately question the very existence of any really immobile boundaries. Astronomy teaches us that the earth itself moves around the sun and that all celestial bodies move at great speed. Nothing seems to be motionless in place. For this reason the term "immobile" should be understood in the sense that the surroundings of an object are *considered* as immobile. In other words, all that is implied is *relative* immobility. As a matter of fact, when we want to indicate the place of an object, we are generally satisfied with giving its position with respect to surroundings that are considered to be fixed.

92. *Reality of Place.* Regarding the question whether place is real, we should distinguish place itself from the being-in-place of a body. Because the place itself of an object is identified with the material surface enclosing the object, it is just as real as this surface itself is real.

The being-in-place of a body, likewise, so it seems, should be considered as a reality and not as a purely extrinsic denomination. If to-be-in-place, just like to be known, were merely a question of naming an object after something extrinsic to it, it would not express a real mode of being. But being-in-place expresses at least that this object exists together with its surroundings, and this real spatial togetherness of distinct beings gives rise to real interrelationships. Thus it would appear that being-in-place is a real mode of being.

93. *Place of the Universe.* The totality of all bodies constituting the universe is not in any place, for the uni-

verse as a whole does not have any surroundings. The same would be true of a body existing without any surroundings or a body that is fully isolated from any surroundings. Like the universe itself, such a body would not be anywhere. Place, therefore, is not an absolute property of material being, but only a property flowing from this being's relations with other bodies.

Absolute Locomotion. A consequence of these assertions is that absolute locomotion of such a body is a contradiction in terms. Locomotion is a passing from one place to another. Evidently, a body that is not in any place cannot move from one place to another. The same applies to the universe as a whole, for it too is not in any place.

Of course, one could *imagine* that such a body or the universe as a whole would proceed to a portion of space where previously nothing was. In this way the body would be considered located and moving relative to this imagined space. However, as we shall see in the next chapter, this imaginary space does not really exist and consequently there can be no question of real locomotion with respect to it.

The objection[2] could be raised that a body moving under the impulse imparted by an external force would keep moving even if the whole surrounding world were suddenly annihilated. Locomotion, therefore, would continue. The reply is that it would continue if it were possible under the stipulated conditions. All the other necessary conditions for locomotion would be present, except that there is no place to move to. But the absence of this *sine qua non* condition renders real motion impossible. On the other hand, it would not be correct to say that the body in question stays in the same place. Since it exists all by itself without any surroundings, the whole concept of

---

[2]Cf. Nys, *Cosmology,* Milwaukee, 1942, vol. II. no. 382.

place has lost its real meaning. The impulse imparted to it would continue to exist in it, but without producing locomotion because one of the necessary conditions for locomotion would not be fulfilled.

Our mind may have difficulty grasping these assertions because our imagination creates space all around the lone body and thus supplies the missing condition. However, this space is not real, so that one of the conditions for locomotion remains absent.

In another sense still locomotion is relative—namely insofar as *mathematically* it makes little difference whether we describe the changing local relationship of A and B by saying that A moves with respect to B or that B moves with respect to A. However, from the ontological point of view, A and B cannot be interchanged indiscriminately, as soon as an exercise of causality is involved. If the cause acts only on A and not on B, then we may not simply substitute B for A. Finally, all locomotion will be purely relative if the whole universe does not contain a single absolutely motionless point of reference.

2. IMPENETRABILITY AND MULTILOCATION

94. *Impenetrability.* Can two or more bodies be present in one and the same place at the same time? The question is not whether some bodies, e.g., sponges, can soak up foreign materials into their pores, but whether a place which is actually and fully occupied by one body in such a way that its dimensions coincide with the dimensions of this body can be simultaneously occupied by another body in the same way.

All will readily agree that experience does not show us any case in which a body occupies a place that is already occupied by another object. To occupy such a place the body always has to dislodge the object and make it change its place. Thus it appears that to the extent that nature is known to us, two bodies are not in the same place. The reason for this physical impenetrability should be sought in the active resistance one body offers to its penetration by another, for this body produces in the other an effect—namely, that of keeping it in another place.

May we go a step further and claim that it is *metaphysically* impossible for two bodies to occupy the same place? Such a conclusion could not follow from the data of experience. To justify it, one would have to show that mutual compenetration is a contradiction in terms. This contradiction would exist if being extended were wholly identical with being impenetrable. If, however, as we asserted above, impenetrability results from the active resistance a body offers to another's penetration, there appears to be no contradiction in the simultaneous presence of two bodies in one place. All that has to be done to produce such a presence is to overcome or rather render inoperative the active resistance proper to a body. Although we have no physical means to render this resistance inoperative, it does not follow therefore that we are faced here with a metaphysical impossibility.[3]

*The objection could be raised that, if compenetration were possible, two straight lines connecting A and B could exist without coinciding, which is impossible. The reply is that two *mathematical* lines would have to coincide. The only reason why mathematical lines are distinct lies in their position; hence if their position is identical, as is asserted in this objection, the two lines must necessarily coincide. However, the same conclusion does not follow with respect to physical bodies, because their distinction does not consist solely in having a different position.[4]

---

[3] The point has some value with respect to certain supernatural phenomena. Christ, for instance, after His resurrection passed through closed doors into the room where the Apostles were gathered. However, such phenomena do not necessarily have to be explained by means of compenetration.

[4] Cf. St. Thomas, *Quodlibet* I, g. 10, a.2, *ad* 2.

95. *Multilocation.* By this term is meant the simultaneous presence of one body in two or more distinct places. Before examining whether such a presence is possible, we must point out that there are various ways in which a being can be present in a place. First of all, a presence may be *circumscriptive*—namely, when a body is present in a place in such a way that its dimensions touch or coincide with the dimensions of the place it occupies and each part of the body is in touch with a different part of the whole place. This kind of being in a place, which is the presence proper to bodies, was the one we had in mind when in the preceding pages we spoke of being in place. Another way of being present is *non-circumscriptively*. We may distinguish two cases here. Something is present wholly in the whole place and wholly in each part of the place. In this way the substantial form, for instance, is present in a body.[5] It is called being present *in the manner of a substance.* Secondly, a being may be present somewhere insofar as it can operate in that place—whence we speak of an *operative* presence. A case in point would be the action of a pure spirit or God on a body.

After these distinctions let us ask the question again: can a body be simultaneously present in two or more places or is such a presence a contradiction in terms? With respect to simultaneous circumscriptive presence the reply is that it would be a metaphysical impossibility. To be circumscriptively present *here* means that the body is located here. If at the same time it were also *there,* then it would be at a distance from itself, which is impossible. Moreover, what is circumscribed by this place is here in such a way that nothing of it is not here; hence it cannot be also there.

However, if the question is asked whether a body can be circumscriptively present in one place and non-circum-

_____

[5]Cf. the author's *Animate Nature,* no. 34.

scriptively elsewhere, then there is no reason why a metaphysical impossibility or internal contradiction should be asserted.[6]

*Historical Notes

96. Although the ideas of place proposed by *Aristotle* and his medieval followers contain many assertions based on antiquated physics, such as the immobility of the earth and the natural place of elements, their philosophical description of place is still valid.

The reality of being in place or ubication is disputed by *Hoenen,* who sees it as a purely extrinsic denomination which does not modify the located object.

The existence of absolute motion and place was defended by *Isaac Newton* (1642-1727), while their essential relativity was stressed by *Descartes.* For *Aristotle* motion could be absolute because he saw the center of the earth as the absolutely immobile reference point of the whole universe.

Descartes rejected the circumscriptive presence of two bodies in one place as a contradiction in terms, for in his view the very essence of a body consisted in its extension. Others, such as *Thomas Aquinas* and *Newton,* saw it only as a physical impossibility. Many philosophers, e.g., *Suarez* and *Descartes* conceive the mutual impenetrability of bodies as a formal consequence of extension, while others, such as *Scotus, Kant,* and *Hoenen* (born 1880), seek its foundation in the active resistance a body offers to other bodies.

Circumscriptive multilocation is commonly rejected by all. But opinions differ as to whether such a multilocation

---

[6]Consequently, such a mixed form of being present in different ways may be used to explain historically verified cases in which persons were seen in different places at the same time and also to remove any semblance of contradiction from the Holy Eucharist in which the body of Jesus Christ is said to be simultaneously present in every consecrated host and in heaven.

would be a contradiction in terms or merely a physical impossibility. *Thomas Aquinas* considers it as a contradiction, but *Scotus* and *Suarez* admit only a physical impossibility.

SUMMARY

97. Place indicates where an object is in reference to others. If the place belongs to several distinct objects, it is called their common place; if it is particular to a single object it is called its proper place. Proper place may be described as the innermost immobile boundary of what immediately surrounds a body. In this description the term *immobile* should be understood in a formal sense, i.e., insofar as it indicates a definite position in the world.

Relative immobility is sufficient for the determination of place, for it allows us to fix the position of an object with respect to surroundings whose local relationships do not change.

Place itself is really identical with the material surface enclosing a body and therefore just as real as this surface itself. With respect to the being-in-place of an object, it seems to be real, for it expresses the real being-together of distinct beings.

The universe itself is not in any place, because it does not have any surroundings. The same would be true for any fully isolated body. The very concept of place becomes meaningless with respect to both cases. Consequently, the same has to be affirmed of the absolute locomotion of the universe as a whole or of the fully isolated body. All locomotion will be purely relative unless one admits the existence of an absolute frame of reference. Locomotion is relative also in the sense that mathematically it makes little difference whether A moves with respect to B or B with respect to A. Physically, however, motion is not relative in this way, for motion implies exercise of causality in the object that is moving or being moved.

Experience does not show any bodies compenetrating one another, so that no two bodies are in the same place. However, compenetration does not seem to be a contradiction in terms, for to be extended is not the same as to be impenetrable. The ontological foundation of impenetrability may be sought in the active resistance one body offers to its penetration by another.

Circumscriptive multilocation of a body is a contradiction in terms, for it would mean that a body which is wholly encompassed by this place is at the same time not wholly encompassed by it. However, no such metaphysical impossibility can be asserted with respect to circumscriptive location in one place and non-circumscriptive location in another.

SUGGESTED READINGS

98. Aristotle, *Physica* bk. IV, chs. 1-6.

Thomas Aquinas, *Comment.* in IV Physica, lect. 1-8.

Andrew G. van Melsen, *Philosophy of Nature,* ch. V, sect. 2.

P. Hoenen, *Cosmologia,* nos. 53-63; Notae IV-VI.

See also the SUGGESTED READINGS after Chapter Nine.

CHAPTER NINE

SPACE

1. ABSOLUTE OR IMAGINARY SPACE

99. *Meanings of the Term "Space".* The word "space" may be taken to mean the dimensions of extension in length, width, and depth. As such, it is real insofar as this extension really exists. As should be clear from the preceding chapters, extension is real insofar as it pertains to a concrete continuous material being.

Secondly, space is often spoken of as if it were a general receptacle or container in which all bodies are located. It is conceived as an immobile extended whole, without limits in any direction, which does not depend on any bodies for its existence, but is uncreated and indestructible, because it remains even if all bodies are thought away. This space is usually called absolute or imaginary space.

The question which we have to examine here is what kind of a being imaginary space is. Is it a reality in itself or not? And if not, is it a pure figment of the mind and the imagination or does it have a foundation in reality?

100. *Absolute Space is Not Real.* To be real, absolute space would have to be an extended being, for it is supposed to contain all bodies, and bodies are extended. But, just like other extended beings, absolute space would need a container, and so on to infinity. Consequently, no space could ever really be the general receptacle of all bodies.

Moreover, from general metaphysical principles it follows that whatever is uncreated is really identical with God. But, unlike extended beings, God does not have any parts. Therefore, absolute space cannot be identical with God.

Thus we may say that absolute or imaginary space exists only in the mind, i.e., is a logical being. Psychologically speaking, the origin of this logical being results from a process of abstraction. The mind eliminates from perceived extended realities all differentiating characteristics and retains only abstract extension as something that stretches off in all directions without any limit.

101. *Absolute Space is Not a Purely Logical Being.* When absolute space is called a logical being, one should keep in mind that there are two kinds of logical beings. Some are purely logical while others have a foundation in reality. Purely logical beings are arbitrarily formed mental constructs which do not contribute anything to our understanding of reality, such as a square circle or a stick with only one end. Reality does not give us any reason to conceive such beings. On the other hand, a logical being may have a foundation in reality. This will be the case if reality itself is the reason why we speak of a non-existent thing as if it were a real being. For instance, a dentist speaks about a cavity as if it existed in a tooth. In reality, however, a cavity does not exist, for a cavity is a negation or absence of dental material in a part of the tooth where this material ought to be present. But there really exist teeth suffering from such absences and for this reason the dentist speaks about cavities as if they were real beings.

With respect to space there is reason for speaking about it *as if* it were real. There exist real bodies characterized by real extension in length, width, and depth. Our mind abstracts these extensions, unites them into a uniform "space," and projects this space without the bodies as if it existed in itself outside the mind. It does not do so arbitrarily but for the purpose of expressing objective reality. For instance, by means of this space it can describe how bodies can successively occupy new parts of space and how new bodies can be added to the existing ones without compressing the bodies that are already in "space." Accordingly, although absolute space is not real, the mind does not speak about it without reason as if it were a real being.

*2. BODIES AND SPACE OF MORE OR LESS THAN THREE DIMENSIONS

102. Space, as we experience it, has three dimensions, and all physical bodies known to us are extended in length, depth, and width. The question may be raised, however, whether beings of a different number of dimensions, are possible.

Beings and Space of One or Two Dimensions. With Henri Poincaré[1] one could "imagine a world uniquely peopled by beings of no thickness (height), and suppose that these 'infinitely flat' animals are all in the same plane and cannot get out . . . While making hypotheses, it costs us no more to endow these beings with reason and believe them capable of creating a geometry. In that case, they will certainly attribute to space only two dimensions." Of course, no one asserts that such beings really exist, but the question may be asked whether these beings and their two-dimensional space are possible or a contradiction in terms.

The mere fact that such beings can be "imagined" evidently does not prove that they are *physically* possible. On the other hand, there appears to be no reason why we should say that they are *metaphysically* impossible. Although it is true that we commonly conceive the two-dimensional plane as the boundary of a body in our three-dimensional world, it does not appear that by intrinsic necessity a plane can exist only as such a boundary and

---

[1]*Science and Hypothesis,* New York, 1952, p. 37.

that, consequently, a two-dimensional world would be a contradiction in terms.

The same line of reasoning applies to the possibility of a one-dimensional world. The answer, then, to the question has to be negative in the sense that we cannot positively affirm the possibility of extended real beings having less than three dimensions, but at the same time we have no reason why we should deny their possibility. All we can say is that such beings do not appear to be metaphysically impossible.

103. *Beings of Four or More Dimensions.* In asking whether extended beings of four or more dimensions can exist, we do not refer to the possibility or usefulness of describing our world by means of four "dimensions." We are solely concerned with the problem whether a world is possible that is circumscribed by four dimensions.

In favor of such a world one could argue in the following ways. Just as a three-dimensional sphere arises from the motion of a two-dimensional plane around a one-dimensional axis, so a four-dimensional figure would arise from the motion of a three-dimensional sphere around a two-dimensional "axis." Or, just as two symmetric triangles cannot coincide in the same plane, but can coincide if one is allowed to use the third dimension for making an 180 degree turn, so also two symmetric solids (e.g., two hands) cannot coincide in three-dimensional space but could coincide if one is allowed to use a fourth dimension for making an analogous kind of "turn."

It should be clear, however, that such statements do not prove the existence or even the possibility of four-dimensional bodies, for they do not prove that it is possible for bodies to move in the prescribed way. Of course, the statements may be useful for mathematicians who want to construct systems in which the properties of such four-dimensional bodies are described, but there is no positive proof that bodies of four dimensions are possible.

111

On the other hand, it is obvious that we cannot conclude from this lack of positive proof to the metaphysical impossibility of such bodies. True, our imagination does not see any other direction than length, width, and depth in which a body can be extended. But this does not prove that such a direction is impossible, but merely that we cannot imagine it. Keeping in mind that our imagination takes all its cognitive elements from the senses and that we have never sensed more than three dimensions, it should not surprise us that we cannot imagine a four-dimensional being. All we can say is that the possibility of such a being has neither been proved nor metaphysically disproved. The same *a fortiori* applies to beings of five or more dimensions.[2]

104. A Boundless but Finite Universe. An interesting problem connected with the foregoing considerations is whether our world could possibly exist in so-called "curved space." To explain what this means, we may use a comparison.[3] The surface of a sphere is without limits in the sense that one may go forward on it without ever coming to the end. On the other hand, this surface is not infinite but finite, for in going forward in a "straight" line (i.e., along the same circle), one will eventually return to the starting point. In other words, we have to do here with a boundless but finite figure. The reason for this apparent paradox is that the sphere curves in the third dimension. For an imaginary two-dimensional being living on such a surface as its universe, its two-dimensional space would be infinite, although it is finite from a tri-dimensional viewpoint because of its curvature. In a similar way, if our tri-dimensional world were bounded by a fourth dimension, it would be infinite from our tri-dimensional viewpoint, but finite insofar as "curves" in the fourth dimension.

---

[2] Cf. Hoenen, *Cosmologia*, Nota VII.
[3] Cf. Poincaré *Science and Hypothesis, loc. cit.*

Space

Such an hypothesis may not be simply rejected as absurd. On the other hand, it appears impossible to obtain an experimental proof, for we cannot travel in a "straight" line around our tri-dimensional world to see if we will ever return to our starting point.

*HISTORICAL NOTES

105. The notion of space has given rise to many divergent views in the course of history, of which we can mention only a few. *Samuel Clarke* (1675-1729) and probably also *Newton* identified space with God's immensity. The ancient atomists, such as *Democritus* (born 540 B. C.) and *Epicurus* (341 ?-270 B. C.), followed by *Gassendi* (1592-1655), appear to have considered space as a reality existing independently of all bodies.

Most philosophers, however, such as *Thomas Aquinas, Kant,* and *Leibniz,* conceive absolute space as a logical being, although they differ on the question whether and to what extent it has a real foundation. For *Kant* it was without any objective basis but merely a subjective form of perception; for *Leibniz* it was nothing but the mutual relationships of bodies. Scholastic philosophers admit that absolute space has a basis in reality but differ in assigning its foundation.

Descartes identified space with extension, which for him was the essence of matter, and thus was forced to deny the possibility of a vacuum.

The question of metageometric space arose in the nineteenth century from the mathematical research of *Nicolai Lobatchewsky* (1793-1856) and *Bernhard Riemann* (1826-1866). *Johann Zöllner* (1834-1882) defended the real existence of four-dimensional space, but others are satisfied with considering it as a mathematical hypothesis of greater or lesser usefulness.

SUMMARY

106. Space is often spoken of as if it were a general receptacle in which all bodies are located. As such, it is conceived as an unlimited and immobile extended whole which does not depend on any bodies for its existence, but is uncreated and indestructible. It is called absolute or imaginary space.

Absolute space is not a real being for, being extended, it itself would need a space as its receptacle, and so on to infinity. Moreover, being uncreated, it would have to be identical with God. This is impossible, for unlike extended space, God does not have any parts. Therefore, absolute space is not a real but a logical being.

On the other hand, absolute space is not a logical being without a foundation in reality. It is not an arbitrarily formed concept, such as a square circle, but serves to express objective reality. By means of this space man can express how bodies can occupy new parts of space and how new bodies may be added to the world without compressing the existing bodies.

*There appears to be no reason why we should say that space and extended beings of less than three dimensions are impossible. The possibility of a world of four or more spatial dimensions is not proved by the supposition of a tri-dimensional body turning around a two-dimensional axis, for the possibility of such a motion is not proved. On the other hand, there appears to be no reason why such a world should be declared a metaphysical impossibility.

*If there exists a fourth dimension, our tri-dimensional universe may be unbounded and at the same time finite, because it could make a "curve" in the fourth dimension. Our situation would be comparable to that of a two-dimensional being living on the surface of a sphere, for which space would be infinite from the two-dimensional

Space

viewpoint, although it is finite from the tri-dimensional stand point.

SUGGESTED READINGS

107. Aristotle, *Physica,* bk. IV, chs. 6-9 (the vacuum).

Thomas Aquinas, *Comment. in VIII Physic.,* bk. IV, lect. 6.

P. Hoenen, *Cosmologia,* nos. 64-70 and *Nota* VII.

Andrew G. van Melsen, *The Philosophy of Nature,* ch 5, sect. 2, pp. 159-163.

Henry J. Koren, *Readings in the Philosophy of Nature:*

Désiré Nys, *The Aristotelian-Thomistic Concept of Space,* pp. 250 ff.

Isaac Newton, *Space, Time, and Motion,* pp. 261 ff.

Edwin A. Burtt, *Criticism of Newton's Philosophy of Space and Time,* pp. 265 ff.

Immanuel Kant, *Space,* pp. 269 ff.

Désiré Nys, *Analysis of Kant's Arguments for Space,* pp. 280 ff.

Max Jammer, *Concepts of Space,* Cambridge, 1954.

Henri Poincaré, *Science and Hypothesis,* New York, 1952, ch. IV.

Vincent E. Smith, *Philosophical Physics,* New York, 1950, ch. 10.

Philipp Frank, *Philosophy of Science,* Englewood Cliffs, 1957 chs. 3 and 10.

See also the Suggested Readings at the end of Chapter Ten.

CHAPTER TEN

TIME

1. THE CONCEPT OF TIME

108. Most people will agree with Saint Augustine's famous statement about time: "If no one asks me about it, I know [what it is], but as soon as I try to explain it to a questioner, I do not know it."[1] Despite this difficulty, we may attempt to investigate the philosophical nature of time and examine some of the difficulties flowing from the so-called relativity of time. Let us begin with a simple question which leads to a suitable description of time.

Description of Time. If someone asks me when Pope Pius XII died, I would reply: on October 9th, 1958, at 3:52 A.M. Usually such an answer will satisfy the questioner. Let us suppose, however, that he inquires further by saying: What do you mean by the number 1958 and all the other numbers? We would have to point out that the first figure is the ordinal number assigned to the revolution of the earth around the sun which was going on when Pius XII died—namely the 1958th revolution since the birth of Christ. To explain the other figures, we would have to add that the 1958th revolution was completing the tenth of the twelve portions (months) into which we have divided each revolution, that the earth was making its ninth rotation around its axis during this portion when Pius XII died, that this rotation had reached the fourth of the twenty-four parts (hours) into which it is divided, and that the fifty-second portion (minute) of this part had just been reached.

---

[1] *Confessions,* bk. XI, ch. 14.

By means of these ordinal numbers anyone knows immediately whether what happened during the revolution indicated by number 1956 occurred before the Pope's death or after it, for the numbers 1956 and 1958 express the relative order of "before" and "after" proper to the parts of time they indicate.

In this way we see that there is an intimate connection between time and motion and that we designate time by the relative motion of the earth and the sun. Thus we can understand why time is described as *motion insofar as it is numbered* or, as Aristotle expresses it, "the number of motion with respect to 'before' and 'after'."[2] For a clearer understanding of this description some supplementary considerations are necessary.

109. *Analogy of Time with Place and Space.* Time has certain features that are analogous with place and space. First of all, place, space, and time all refer to something *continuous*. The difference is that the continuity of space and place is fixed, while that of time is fluid, for it is the continuity proper to motion.

Secondly, in both space and time we may speak of *"before"* and *"after."* For instance, travelling from New York to San Francisco, Chicago is reached before San Francisco, but after Cleveland. In time, 1956 comes before 1957 but after 1955. There is a difference, however, between the spatial and temporal "before" and "after." If instead of travelling from New York to San Francisco, I travel from San Francisco to New York, Chicago is no longer "after" Cleveland but "before" it. In other words, the spatial "before" and "after" are relative to the freely chosen starting point. The same relativity, however, does not apply to the temporal "before" and "after," because there is no possibility of reversing the course of time in

---

[2]*Physica*, bk. IV, ch. 11, 220a 24.

reality. Consequently, the order of priority and posteriority is essential to time.

Thirdly, in space we may speak of a *topological* and a *metric* structure. The first of these terms refers to the place occupied by a body in reference to others (e.g., in Chicago) ; the second indicates how much space a body occupies or its distance from another body (e.g., ten cubic feet or 300 miles from Chicago). Similar structures are found in time. When we say, for instance, that World War I took place before World War II, we refer to the topological structure of time, which corresponds with place; and when we mention that the trip to New York took us nine hours, we make reference to the metric structure of time, which corresponds with space.[3]

110. *Time and Motion.* As was mentioned above, time and motion are intimately connected. Both have the nature of a fluid continuum in the sense that only their actual moment or phase exists and that their other parts are no longer or not yet. Time without motion is not conceivable, for if there is no motion at all, there is no succession but only unvaried existence.

Any kind of successive motion, e.g., a change in intensity, has the aspect of time, for the succession can be numbered. However, locomotion is always given preference because it is easier to see what time is by means of this kind of motion.

With respect to the successive motion of an object, we may distinguish the starting point, the terminus, and the intermediary continuous distance. This continuous distance or road to be travelled has (potential) parts that are successively traversed in going from the starting point to the terminus. We can discern many parts in this distance

---

[3]The numbers used in referring to the metric structure of time are no longer mere ordinal numbers but have a cardinal value insofar as they indicate equal parts of time measured by a uniform motion.

and distinguish them by designating them by a sequence of numbers. In this way these numbers become the numbers of the motion in question. What is meant by time is precisely motion insofar as it is numbered or at least can be numbered in this way.

*The objection could be raised that numbers indicate discrete quantity, while time is continuous. The reply is that the term "number" should not be understood here as the abstract or "numbering" numbers by which we count—otherwise every number would be time—but the concrete parts of motion that are counted. These parts are referred to as "numbered" numbers. Hence, just as we use numbers to indicate the parts of a continuous body, so also may we use numbers to refer to the parts of a continuous motion.

Measurement of Time. As was pointed out above, time is used not only to indicate the relative temporal position of events, but also the duration of something. When we speak of the duration of something or the temporal distance of two events, we refer to the metric structure of time. This duration or distance can be measured insofar as the beginning and end of a duration or the position of two events are simultaneous with two phases of the continuous motion that serves to measure time. To be of practical value for measuring time, the motion in question should be uniform, for otherwise its various parts would not correspond to equal distances; it should be periodic, so that it is relatively easy to discern its parts, for otherwise it cannot serve as a standard of measurement; finally, it should be general enough to extend to all things whose time we want to measure. This ideal motion is sufficiently approached by the earth's rotation around its axis and its revolution around the sun. For this reason we place events in time and measure the duration of objects by means of the numbers assigned to the parts of the earth's motion.

119

111. *Time and Duration.* The concept of duration is broader than that of time. Duration indicates continuous existence or persistence in being. It does not add anything real to existence but merely implies that an existing reality continues to be itself. Consequently, there are as many ways of perduring as there are modes of remaining identical with itself.

We may distinguish three types of duration. With respect to God, duration is totally devoid of any change of identity. He perdures forever as fully identical with Himself. The very idea of succession is utterly foreign to His nature, so that the concept of time cannot in any way apply to Him. His duration is *eternity* which, according to Boethius' classical definition, is described as the simultaneous and complete possession of unending life.

Finite beings, on the other hand, do not perdure in full identity with themselves. They are characterized by a succession of changes, so that in one way or another the idea of temporality applies to them. Nevertheless, not all finite beings are temporal in exactly the same sense. Some perdure without being subject to any change in their essential mode of being because their essence is simple and without any composition. Such beings, therefore, in their essence are always fully identical with themselves. Moreover, once they are, they are forever, and in this sense they may be said to participate to some extent in God's eternal duration. On the other hand, their essence is not their action, so that we may speak of a succession of activities in such beings. Accordingly, temporality applies to them only with respect to their secondary modes of being. A duration which is characterized by essential self-identity coupled with accidental successive changes is called an *"eviternity."* It is proper to created immaterial beings.

Finally there are material beings whose very essence is subject to change. They are not even what they essentially are fully at once but only successively and transitorily. Their duration is that of *time*.

2. THE REALITY OF TIME

112. In speaking about the reality of time, we should make a distinction between absolute time and "real" time.

Absolute Time. Absolute or imaginary time is analogous with absolute or imaginary space. It is supposed "to flow equably without relation to anything external,"[4] without beginning or end, uncreated and indestructible, as a kind of general receptacle in which all motions take place, just as space is the general receptacle in which all extended beings are located.

This imaginary time is not real. It is conceived as a continuous motion and, therefore, it would need a receptacle just as the other motions are supposed to need one. Consequently, we would have here the same process to infinity as in imaginary space. Moreover, as uncreated, it would have to be really identical with God, which is impossible.[5]

Accordingly, absolute time exists only in the mind as a logical being. Psychologically speaking, the idea of such an imaginary time arises from a process of abstraction by which the mind strips motion of all individually characteristics and retains only fluid continuity conceived as stretching without beginning and end.

However, the mind does not conceive such a being without reason, but uses it to express certain truths. For instance, if it is true, as is sometimes asserted, that our universe came into existence five billion years ago, we may ask: could another universe have existed, say, ten billion years ago? Or, can another come into existence a billion years later if ours were to be annihilated? These questions are analogous to those asking whether there is space available for additional bodies outside our universe.

---

[4]Newton, *Mathematical Principles of Natural Philosophy,* Berkeley, 1946, p. 6.
[5]Cf. above, no. 100.

They may be answered in the affirmative, for all they mean is whether the existence of another universe than ours is possible. Because absolute time aids us in expressing this truth, it is a logical being with a foundation in reality.

113. *"Real" Time.* By "real time" we mean time insofar as it is an aspect of real continuous motion and not of the imaginary motion that gives rise to the concept of absolute time.

At first sight it may seem that this "real" time can exist only in the mind. The parts of time are past and future, separated by an indivisible present. But the past is no longer, and the future is not yet. Only the present instant is, but it alone is not time.

Nevertheless, we may affirm that this time is real and not only an object of the mind. Time is the number of motion. But motion is numbered independently of the mind's consideration. As was pointed out before, number should not be understood here as the abstract or "numbering" number which evidently can exist only in the numbering mind, but as the concrete or "numbered" number. Whether or not anyone counts how many bricks there are in a house, a certain number applies to the collection of bricks, and in this sense they are concretely numbered.

The objection could be raised that there is no parity between the bricks of a house and the parts of motion because the bricks actually exist together while the parts of a motion do not exist actually but only potentially. In other words, the parts of motion are not numbered but only *numerable* and therefore require to be actually counted by an intellect. Consequently, time does not exist independently of the mind.

We may reply by pointing out that the numerability of motion is sufficient to safeguard the reality of time. This numerability implies order in respect of "before" and "after" and, consequently, can function as the principle

by which motion is temporally measured. Whether anyone actually counts or measures does not change the nature
of this measuring principle, but merely refers to its application. On the other hand, it is evident that the application of this measure is not independent of the mind.

Regarding the objection that only the indivisible present
exists, while the past and the future are not now, it is to
be noted that in a way the present includes the past and
the future, just as motion in any of the points it traverses
implies its preceding and succeeding phases. The present
would not be present if there had been no past and would
be no future. Without the past, the present would merely
be the beginning of time; without the future, the present
would be nothing but the end of time. Thus, although it
is true that time is actual only in an indivisible now, its
past and future are contained in the present insofar as the
present is meaningless and inconceivable without the past
and the future.

3. TIME AND RELATIVITY

114. Before considering a few of the so-called philosophical consequences of the relativity theory, we will first
express the pertinent points of this difficult mathematico-
physical theory in the simplest possible way and describe
in a few words the revolution it has caused in modern
physics.

The Classical Principle of Relativity. If a ball is
dropped in a moving train, the passenger sees it fall to
the ground in a vertical line. For another observer, however, who is standing alongside the tracks, the falling ball
describes a parabola. The reason why the two do not
agree in their description of the event is that their frames
of references are not the same; the passenger describes the
motion in reference to the moving train, and the other
observer speaks about it in reference to the earth. In other

words, the path of the motion is relative to the frame of reference or, to use more mathematical terms, the system of co-ordinates.

To describe the motion more fully, we would have to indicate how the position of the reference frame changes with time. By means of two identically constructed clocks —one in the train and the other alongside the tracks—the passenger and the observer could determine what position the ball has at each tick of the clock.

The relativity of motion described in the foregoing paragraphs is expressed by the classical or Newtonian principle of relativity. It asserts that the states of rest and uniform rectilinear motion of a system are irrelevant with respect to the mechanical events occurring in this system.

Propagation of Light. If a passenger walks forward with a speed of three miles an hour in reference to a train doing sixty miles an hour, then he is moving with a velocity of 63 miles an hour in reference to the tracks. If the sun is taken as the point of reference, his speed is different because we have to take into consideration the velocity with which the earth turns around the sun. A fourth velocity is obtained when we take the "fixed" stars as our system of reference. These additions (or subtractions) of speed that have to be made are examples of the so-called Galileo transformation, a formula used in classical mechanics to determine the velocity of a moving body with respect to a system of reference.

A difficulty, however, arises with respect to the propagation of light. Light moves with a constant velocity, whether or not it travels in the same direction as the source of light. But according to the classical principle of relativity, the velocity of a light signal travelling (in a vacuum) in the same direction as a passenger on a train moving one kilometer per second should be 300,000—1 km. or 299,999 km. as seen from the train. In other words, light seems to disobey the Galileo transformation.

115. *Special Theory of Relativity.* To solve this difficulty, Albert Einstein (1879-1955) formulated the special theory of relativity. Its fundamental ideas are the following:

1. *Relativity of Time.* Simultaneity has no absolute meaning but is relative to the frame of reference. If two lights, *A* and *B,* which are ten miles apart, simultaneously send signals to an observer stationed midway at *M* between them, he would see the flashes of *A* and *B* at the same time. But another observer aboard a speeding train, travelling parallel to the path of the light rays towards *B,* who is exactly at *M* when the flashes occur, will see flash *B* before flash *A.* For he is approaching *B* and receding from *A,* so that the light from *A* has to travel a longer distance than the light from *B.* In other words, events that are simultaneous with respect to an inert frame of reference (the tracks) are not simultaneous with respect to a moving frame of reference (the train).

2. *Relativity of Distance.* The length of a body or the distance of its two extremes has no absolute value but depends on the frame of reference. The length of a moving train, as measured within the train itself, does not necessarily coincide with the same distance or length measured outside the train on the tracks. To determine the outside distance we would indicate two points of the track that are reached simultaneously, in reference to the tracks, by the front and the rear of the train. But these two points are not necessarily reached simultaneously also as judged by the passenger who takes the train as his system of reference. In other words, distance and length are relative to the frame of reference.

Certain phenomena of experience can be explained only if we admit that the faster a body moves, the shorter it becomes in the direction of its motion. A measuring rod, for example, is longer when at rest than when in motion, and a clock goes slower in a moving reference system than in a system at rest.

Because classical relativity does not take into consideration that both distance and time vary when they are measured in reference to a moving system or a system at rest, the velocity of light does not obey the Galileo transformation of velocities. But if the Galileo formula is replaced by a more accurate formula (the Lorentz transformation) in which these changing factors are taken into account, the difficulty vanishes and the speed of light remains constant.

Accordingly, space and time should not be treated as distinct entities, for they fuse together into a single space-time continuum of four dimensions in which the various beings of the world are located.

116. *General Theory of Relativity.* Einstein's special theory of relativity applies only to reference bodies in a so-called inertial system, i.e., a system in which bodies are either in a state of rest or of uniform rectilinear motion. In a few words, it states that for the physical description of the general laws of nature, such as those of mechanics and the propagation of light, a reference body at rest does not have more value than one in uniform rectilinear motion.

The general theory of relativity extends his principles to all reference bodies, whether their motion is uniform and rectilinear or non-uniform and non-rectilinear, e.g., accelerated and curvilinear.

To use an example, if a stone is released from our grasp, it falls to the ground. The classical explanation of this phenomenon is that it is attracted by the gravitational force of the earth. But, according to Einstein, this statement is an explanation in terms of a particular body of reference. If instead of the stone falling down, the earth is considered to move upwards with the same speed as we ascribe to the stone, exactly the same effect would be seen by the earthly observer.

To clarify the matter by means of an illustration, let us suppose that an elevator cage were situated in space outside the gravitational fields of attraction surrounding stars and planets. Such an elevator would be free from gravitation. If suddenly the elevator cage were pulled upward with a uniformly accelerated motion, the elevator man would experience what we always call gravitation and think that he is pulled downwards by the force of gravity. Any object he releases will appear to descend with a uniformly accelerated motion because of the attraction of a gravitational field. But an independent observer outside the cage would describe the "gravitational pull" as the upward motion of the other's reference system (the elevator cage). Who is right? We may say both, but only with respect to their particular reference system. In other words, what is called the effect of a gravitational field in one reference system may be called the effect of an acceleration in another reference system. Or, to express it more technically, gravitational mass equals inertial mass. Therefore, instead of saying that the passenger in the train lurches forward when the brakes are applied, we may just as well say that under the influence of a gravitational field the tracks and the earth move forward with a non-uniform accelerated motion, while the train itself remains at rest.

117. The *consequences of the relativity theory* that have to be considered here are the following:

1. Does the theory of relativity make all human knowledge purely relative?

2. Since different observers may see the same chain of events in opposite orders, does relativity mean that the order of cause and effect is purely relative and conventional?

3. Is the succession of a chain of events nothing else than a successive observation of timeless events, so that the future is already here?

4. Does relativity justify a fatalistic attitude?

5. Does the theory allow us to ascribe the relative motion of two bodies arbitrarily to either one or the other?

6. Is our universe a four-dimensional space-time continuum?

7. Does relativity prove that there is no objective simultaneity?

8. Is it meaningful to speak about the objective length of a body?

A few words have to be devoted to each of these issues.

Is All Human Knowledge Purely Relative? Although this claim is sometimes made and some philosophers endeavor to do away with all absolute values, such a radical view cannot be based on the relativity theory. At most, one may say that the theory has created a psychological atmosphere which favors attempts to extend its contentions to other realms of human knowledge. But the theory itself is concerned only with the dependence of certain physical measurements, e.g., those of time and distance, on the frames of reference and attempts to find values for these quantities that will remain the same in every frame of reference. In other words, the relativity theory endeavors to find a value which remains absolute, regardless of the frame of reference. Accordingly, instead of making everything relative, the theory is an excellent confirmation of the old metaphysical thesis that all relativity includes something absolute.

118. *Is the Order of Cause and Effect Made Purely Conventional?* This assertion is sometimes made, because the theory says that different observers may see the same chain of events in opposite orders. However, such a view is based on a misinterpretation of relativity. The theory claims merely that *causally unrelated* events may appear in different orders to different observers and not that the order of causally connected events can be inverted. All that can happen with respect to causally related events is that the time interval between them appears shorter or longer according to the reference system used by different observers. No matter, however, what reference system is used, there will always be some interval of time.

The metaphysical reason why no effect can *occur* before its cause is rather obvious: the effect depends on the cause for its coming to be and thus cannot precede it. The physical reason why no effect *appears* before its cause is that the transmission of physical action requires time and no physical action travels faster than light.

119. *Is the Future Already Here?* It is sometimes claimed, e.g., by Sir James Jeans, that according to relativity, time does not have a past, present, and future. A so-called succession of events is nothing but a successive observation of timeless events, so that the future is already here and merely waiting for us to observe it.

Such a view, however, cannot be accepted. The denial of the future arises from the idea that the time-dimension in space-time is of the same nature as the space-dimensions, because time cannot be measured independently of distance (space). But this mathematical procedure should not make us forget that, in opposition to space, time is essentially a *fluid* continuum: it is not given at once in its totality but only successively.

The spatial representation of time by a line in which past events are situated on one side of the point indicating the present and future events on the other powerfully suggests that all these events exist together and that time is merely "our incapacity to know everything at once" (Bergson). But this spatial symbolism of time should not induce us to neglect the qualitative differences of space and time. Space is given at once as a continuous whole with all its parts, but time is given only successively; space is reversible in the sense that one can travel it arbitrarily in all directions, while time is essentially irreversible inasmuch as we cannot travel backward in time.

120. *Does Relativity Favor Fatalism?* From the preceding considerations it follows also that relativity does not prove anything in favor of fatalism. Some people argue: the explosion of this bomb has already happened for one observer at 12:00 o'clock; for a second observer using a different reference system it has not yet happened at 12:00 o'clock, but he is powerless to prevent it because it has already taken place and duly recorded by another observer.

The fallacy of this line of reasoning lies in the way it formulates the events. All the theory of relativity says is that when the explosion occurred, the clock of the first observer showed 12:00 o'clock, but the clock of the second observer, which runs at a greater speed, had reached 12:00 o'clock before the explosion occurred.

121. *Can Motion be Arbitrarily Ascribed to a Particular Body?* Does the theory of relativity make it purely a matter of convention to ascribe the relative motion of two bodies either to one or to the other, because it is impossible to determine whether A moves relative to B or B relative to A?

This point has already been considered in no. 93. From the standpoint of *mathematical* description it may be merely a matter of convenience to ascribe the change of position resulting from motion either to A or to B. However, if the question is considered not only insofar as the mathematical description is concerned, but also with respect to the *causality* that is exercised in motion, the situation is different. If this causality acts only on A and not on B, then to ascribe the motion to A is not a matter of convention but absolutely necessary for the description of motion as it really is. On the other hand, it may be true that in certain cases its is impossible for the human observer to determine whether A moves physically with respect to B or vice versa. In other words, whether the motion is ascribed to A or B may be irrelevant to the mathematical description of physical laws, but the relativity of this description does not justify us in concluding that the causality involved in motion can be arbitrarily said to be exercised on either A or B.

122. *Is Our Universe a Four-Dimensional Continuum of Space-Time?* This question can be understood in several ways. First of all, an affirmative answer may be taken to mean that the totality of all events in the universe is already "there" and that we merely become aware of them in successive "nows." In this case the reply is the same as the assertion that the future exists already. It must be rejected for the reasons given above in no. 119, for it would mean that there is no difference at all between the natures of space and time.

On the other hand, the affirmative answer could be understood in the sense that in describing the events of our physical world we must take into consideration that the measurements of time and distance are not independent or that the physical laws of the universe can be expressed more accurately in terms of a space-time continuum.[6] In this sense there is no objection to the affirmative reply.

---

[6] Because relativity enables the physicist to express his measurements of space and time in a way that is independent of the state of motion of the observer.

123. *Is There No Objective Simultaneity?* Let us point out, first of all, that the relativistic denial of simultaneity does not extend to events occurring *in the same place.* So far as such events are concerned, all admit that they may be simultaneous, no matter what frame of reference is used.

The denial applies only to the simultaneity of distant events. The theory of relativity proves that simultaneity of distant events is *not observable,* because the physical means at our disposal cannot instantaneously inform us of the occurrence of a distant event. It, therefore, justifies the physicist in concluding that this objective simultaneity is meaningless in his science, because his science is limited to conclusions that are verifiable by sense experience.

May we proceed further and say that it proves objective simultaneity meaningless from every point of view and therefore *non-existent?* The reply is in the negative. If there were any signals that could be transmitted instantaneously, the simultaneity of distant events would not only exist but also be observable. In former times the propagation of light and gravitation were thought to be instantaneous. Although we know now that these phenomena have a finite velocity, we may not *a priori* exclude that there exist other physical phenomena which are instantaneous. True, experience offers us no reason to proclaim the existence of such phenomena, but—can science claim that it is omniscient and knows already everything about the physical world? Thus there is no justification for the claim that the relativity theory has positively *disproved* objective simultaneity or even the possibility of its observation.

On the other hand, the absence of this positive proof does not mean that objective simultaneity exists. The burden of proving its existence falls on its proponents, for physical science limits itself to statements that can be verified by sense experience. The question, therefore, is whether or not we can justify the assertion that distant events are simultaneous in an objective or non-relative (though unobservable) way. To say it differently, can we show that my "here-now" coincides with a "there-now" and not merely with a "there-then"?

It is here that most scientist-philosophers part company with their non-scientist colleagues. The latter usually claim that such a simultaneity is an intellectual insight, whereas the former reject this claim and say in all sincerity that they do not have such an insight.

The denial of the scientist-philosophers does not necessarily mean that there is no such insight. Their constant reliance on the observable for the verification of their conclusions may have rendered them psychologically unable to think about nature on a level where no sensible verification is possible. On the other hand, the assertion of the non-scientist philosopher, likewise, is not unconditionally trustworthy, no matter how obvious his proclaimed insight may seem to be. Only too often such alleged insights have shown themselves to be nothing but deeply ingrained customary patterns of thinking.

124. To solve the dilemma, we propose to proceed in the following way. We will first show that, despite their aversion to insights, scientists do not hesitate to rely on them, and then that even the relativists *de facto* admit the meaningfulness of simultaneity with respect to distant events.

The first point may be made clear by means of a few examples. Scientists admit, at least implicitly, many principles that are not based on experimental verification but on intellectual insight. For instance, the principles of contradiction and of sufficient reason; the principle that if a theory disagrees with the facts, we should abandon the theory; the conviction that nature is intelligible, etc. Consequently, no scientist may reject the validity of intellectual insight.

With respect to the second point, if we can show that the relativists themselves *de facto* admit the simultaneity of distant events, then we are in possession of strong evidence in favor of the philosopher's proclaimed insight. There are several ways in which this point can be shown, but we will limit ourselves to one. The relativists say, for instance, that identical processes will develop "faster" or "slower" according to the state of motion in which a body is. This assertion means that a process in one body which starts at the same time as a similar process in another body will take a longer or shorter temporal course to reach its completion, so that the ends of the two processes are not reached at the same time. If the expressions "at the same time" and "not at the same time" are declared to have no objective value, then the whole statement itself would be meaningless, because "faster" would have a changing or relative value and could conceivably become just the opposite. Consequently, it seems that such statements of relativists show that they implicity admit the objectivity of simultaneity even in distant events.[7]

By way of conclusion we may point out that a certain amount of confusion is generated by the term "objective" or "absolute" simultaneity. For the relativistic physicist it means simultaneity which is the same for all observers. In this sense, it must be admitted that no such simultaneity of distant events is known to us. For a realistic philosopher, on the other hand, the term refers to simultaneity "in itself," i.e., the simultaneity of events as they are in reality, independently of observation. This realistic notion, of course, is wholly unacceptable to any philosopher of sci-

---

[7]Cf. Nicolai Hartmann, *Philosophie der Natur,* Berlin, 1950, p. 240. The view that absolute simultaneity is a presupposition of the theory of relativity is held also by others, e.g., Andrew G. van **Melsen and P. Henry van Laer.**

ence who is more or less imbued with positivistic ideas about our inability to know things independently of observation. The justification of realism, however, is a question which lies beyond the scope of the philosophy of nature. It is considered in epistemology.

125. *Is it Meaningful to Speak About the Objective Length of a Body?* When relativists reject the meaningfulness of objective length, they base themselves on the fact that the measurement of length will give different results according to the state of motion of the measuring rod and of the body that is to be measured.

In this point also confusion arises from the use of the term "objective." For the physicist, length is objective when it is absolute, i.e., when its measurement will be the same for all observers. For the philosopher length is objective when it is real, i.e., when it does not exist only in the consideration of the mind. In the first sense of the term one may legitimately claim that objective length is meaningless. But if the term is taken in its philosophical meaning, then the relativity resulting from physical measurements does not allow us to reject the objective reality of a body's length. Objective length in the philosophical sense means that a body has a definite size independently of sense observation.

The assertion that a concretely existing body has a definite size is not based on its measurement or its measurability but on an intellectual insight. This insight teaches us that the extremes of an actually extended body do not coincide but actually have a certain distance between them. This distance cannot be undetermined or indefinite in itself, for otherwise the extremes of the body would be at the same time here (at P and Q) and not here but there (at R and S), which is impossible. Just as an actual crowd objectively consists of a definite number of human beings, even if we are unable to count them, so also a concretely extended body objectively has a definite size even if we have no means of measuring this size in an absolute way.

It should be noted, however, that in attributing a definite objective size to a body, independently of its measurement, we do not at all want to assert that this size remains the same, regardless of the state of motion proper to a body. It may, and as a matter of fact does, stretch and shrink according as the body whose size it is undergoes a change in its state of motion.

*Historical Notes

126. Idealistic trends of philosophy deny the reality of time. *Leibniz* makes it consist in the order the mind imposes on succeeding things. *Kant* reduces it to a mere *a priori* form of sensibility. *Descartes* also conceives time as a mode of thought. For *John Locke* (1632-1704) time is a product of our reflection and therefore purely psychological. *Henri Bergson* distinguishes homogeneous and heterogeneous time. Homogeneous or measurable time is a spatialization of successive states of consciousness and does not really exist. Heterogeneous time or "duration" is the succession of conscious states. This time is real, but it is of a purely qualitative nature and not subject to measurement because consciousness is not extended.

Ultrarealistic views of time consider it an uncreated immaterial reality (*Gassendi,* 1592-1655), a divine attribute (*Clarke*) or, together with space, as the primordial stuff giving rise to the Deity (*Samuel Alexander,* 1859-1938). Although scholastic philosophers generally viewed absolute time and space as mere logical beings, most scientists before *Einstein* followed, at least in practice, *Newton's* exaggerated views of the reality of space and time, stripped of their theological implications. One of Einstein's main contentions in relativity was to show that if matter and its motion disappeared, there would no longer be any space or time.

Aristotle, Thomas Aquinas and many others defend the reality of time in the sense explained in the preceding pages.

SUMMARY

127. Time may be suitably described as motion insofar as it is numbered or as the number of motion with respect to "before" and "after." It shares many features with space. Both are continuous; both admit a "before" and "after"; both have a topological and a metric structure. On the other hand, there are also characteristic differences: the continuity of space is fixed, and that of time is fluid; the "before" and "after" of space are reversible, and that of time is irreversible.

Motion and time have the nature of a fluid continuum insofar as only their actual phase or moment exists. As the number of motion, time is essentially an aspect of motion. Because in any continuous motion there are successive phases, any such motion has the aspect of time. Usually, however, we measure time by means of locomotion. In successive motion we may distinguish the starting point, the terminus, and the intermediary continuous distance to be traversed. The potential parts of this distance are discernible and can be designated by a series of numbers. When we speak about time we mean precisely motion insofar as it can be numbered in this way.

*The number of which there is question in time is not the abstract numbering number but the concrete number of parts of motion.

Time indicates not only the relative position of events but also the duration of something. The duration of an object is measured by the simultaneity of its beginning and end with two phases of the motion by which time is measured. Likewise, the relative position of an event is usually indicated by its simultaneity with a phase of this motion. In practice, the motion used for measuring time is the earth's rotation around its axis and its revolution around the sun because these motions sufficiently approach the ideal of a uniform, periodic and general motion.

Duration is broader than time. It indicates that a thing continues to be itself. The duration of a being that always remains fully identical with itself is called eternity; that of a being which remains essentially itself but changes in its activities is called eviternity; that of a being which is subject to essential change is time.

Absolute time, which is analogous with absolute or imaginary space, is a logical being. It has a foundation in reality insofar as it serves to express the truth than another physical universe could have existed before ours or could come into existence after it.

Time which is an aspect of real continuous motion is real, for independently of the mind's consideration its parts are concretely numbered insofar as the order of its parts is determined by the motion. Although only the indivisible present exists actually, this present, as present, implies the past and the future, for without them the present would be meaningless.

According to the classical principle of relativity, the states of uniform rectilinear motion or of rest of a physical system are irrelevant with respect to the mechanical events occurring in the system. Einstein's special theory of relativity extends this principle to electromagnetic phenomena, and his general theory of relativity enlarges it to include also the state of non-uniform non-rectilinear motion. As a result, the simultaneity or succession of distant events are declared to depend on the reference system used by the observer, for both time and distance vary in different systems of reference and cannot be measured independently.

It is to be noted that this theory does not make all human knowledge relative, but denies only the independent measurability of space and time. It does not abolish the cause and effect relationship of events for it has value only for causally unrelated events. It cannot be interpreted as the abolition of the future, for it does not make time a fixed continuum that is there at once in its totality. Relativity does not favor fatalism but merely asserts that different clocks in different reference systems may not indicate the same time for the same event. It makes the attribution of motion to one body in preference to another a matter of arbitrary convention from the viewpoint of the motion's mathematical description, but not with respect to the causality that is exercised in motion. Relativity makes the universe a four-dimensional continuum in the sense that our description of the world must take into consideration that time and distance cannot be measured independently, but not in the sense that the dimension of time is already there and merely waiting for us to be observed in cross-cuts of the four-dimensional continuum.

The theory does not deny the objective simultaneity of events occurring at the same, place, but asserts that such simultaneity does not exist with respect to distant events, because it is impossible to observe this simultaneity. However, this assertion merely presumes that all the means of observation are already known to us; hence the theory does not even disprove the possibility of observing this simultaneity. As to the objective existence of this simultaneity, the scientist usually denies that it is evident from an immediate philosophical insight, while the non-scientist as a rule asserts the contrary. Without being too hasty in accepting this particular proclaimed insight, we may point out that scientists at least in practice admit the value of certain philosophical insights, e.g., the principles of contradiction, sufficient reason, and the intelligibility of being. Secondly, the relativistic statement that identical processes can develop temporally faster or slower in differently moving bodies, means that if the processes begin at the same time, they do not terminate at the same time. This "same time" cannot be made relative, for otherwise the statement would be meaningless. Consequently, the relativists implicitly admit that distant events may be simultaneous.

While it may be admitted that it is meaningless to speak of the objective length of a body in the physical sense of absolute length, we cannot reject objective length in the philosophical sense as the size a body has in reality independently of our observation. For if the size were indefinite in reality, the extremes of the body would be at the same time here and not here but there, which is impossible.

SUGGESTED READINGS

128. Aristotle, *Physica,* bk IV, chs. 10-14.

Thomas Aquinas, *Comment. in IV Physic.,* lect. 15-23.

P. Hoenen, *Cosmologia,* nos. 170-188.

Andrew G. van Melsen, *The Philosophy of Nature,* ch. V, nos. 4-7, pp. 176-198.

Henry J. Koren, *Readings in the Philosophy of Nature:*

Désiré Nys, *The Aristotelian-Thomistic Theory of Space and Time,* pp. 244 ff.

Isaac Newton, *Space, Time, and Motion,* pp. 261 ff.

Edwin Burtt, *Criticism of Newton's Philosophy of Space and Time,* pp. 265 ff.

Immanuel Kant, *Space and Time,* pp. 269 ff.

Désiré Nys, *Analysis of Kant's Arguments,* pp. 278ff.

Albert Einstein, *Space and Time,* pp. 283 ff.

Milic Capek, *Relativity and the Status of Space,* pp. 290 ff.

Peter Hoenen, *Simultaneity and the Principle of Positivism,* pp. 308 ff.

Philipp Frank, *Is the Future Already Here?* pp. 315 ff.

Lincoln Barnett, *Did the Universe Have a Beginning?* pp. 322 ff.

Vincent Smith, *Philosophical Physics,* ch. 11.

Philipp Frank, *Philosophy of Science,* chs. 5 and 7.

Herbert Dingle, *The Scientific Adventure,* New York, 1953, pp. 215-235.

A. d'Abro, *The Evolution of Scientific Thought,* New York, n.d., Parts II and III.

CHAPTER ELEVEN

QUALITY

129. Philosophy traditionally describes the category of quality as an accident which formally modifies a substance in itself. In a broad sense, however, the term "quality" is used for all kinds of accidents and even for essential characteristics. We are using it here in the strict sense as opposed to substance and to the other accidents. The term "accident" indicates the distinction from substance, "formally" distinguishes quality from quantity, which merely extends the substance, and the words "in itself" set quality apart from the other accidents, which modify the substance not in itself but in reference to something else.

We will consider qualities here only insofar as they pertain to the material world and give rise to philosophical problems. Moreover, not all philosophical questions of quality will be treated here, but only the following:

1. The reality of sense-perceptible qualities;

2. The relationship of quality and quantity;

3. Qualitative change or alteration;

4. Qualities as principles of activity.

1. THE REALITY OF SENSE-PERCEPTIBLE QUALITIES

Meaning of the Term "Sense-Perceptible Quality." The term "sense-perceptible qualities" applies here both to qualities that are immediately perceived by the senses, such as colors and sounds, and to others that do not directly lead to sensations but only to effects which are sense-perceptible. Examples of the latter are chemical properties and magnetism.

According as qualities are immediately perceptible only by one sense or by more than one, they are traditionally called "proper" and "common" sensibles.[1] John Locke, however, introduced the terms "primary" and "secondary" sense qualities. They correspond roughly to common and proper sensibles. Thus color and sound are secondary or proper sense qualities, while motion, rest, and shape exemplify the primary or common type of qualities. As is well-known, Locke denied the real existence of secondary sense qualities and admitted only the objectivity of the primary sensibles. The mechanists also deny all sense qualities except locomotion. Accordingly, although at first sight the existence of sense qualities may seem to be obvious from observation, we will have to investigate whether or not they exist in reality.

In this question, however, we will abstract from the epistemological problem regarding the mode of existence to be attributed to these qualities if their objectivity is admitted. Some assert that they exist formally in reality, so that, say, redness exists as such in a rose, while others attribute to them only a causal or fundamental existence, i.e., there is a quality in the rose which produces in the observer a sensation of redness. All we want to do here is, first, show that proper or secondary sense qualities are real, whatever may be their exact nature, and secondly, that these qualities cannot be simply reduced to locomotion.

130. *The Objectivity of the Proper Sense Qualities.* We may start by assuming that epistemology has validated the existence of a material world that is not merely an object of the mind. In addition, we admit that we sometimes have perceptions to which we refer as sensations of color and sound. Moreover, hardly anyone would object

---

[1]Cf. the author's *Animate Nature*, no. 75.

to the statement that in some way these perceptions are an experience of real modes of being in the sense that they pertain either to the reality of the perceiving subject or to the object perceived. For otherwise these perceptions would have to be manifestations of non-being, which is impossible. The problem, however, is whether these modes of being pertain to the self of the knower or to a non-self, i.e., to a reality that is distinct from the knower.

With respect to this problem, we may argue in the following way. In the knower we distinguish consciousness and the sense organs through which he becomes aware of the sense qualities in question. If the sense qualities are not produced either by consciousness or by the sense organs, then they must be realities that are independent of the knower as such. Now the knower, insofar as he is conscious, is not aware of producing the sense qualities. On the contrary, the qualities force themselves on his perception. The hypothesis that he produces them unconsciously has to admit that they are not the result of his consciousness as such, so that they must be real. The supposition that his sense organs alone produce them does not harmonize with the fact that different sense objects give rise to different perceptions of sense qualities. Therefore, there must be something outside the sense organs and outside consciousness, i.e., in a reality, distinct from the knower, which leads to these perceptions of sense qualities. Consequently, the sense qualities are real.

131. *Material Qualities are Not Simply Reducible to Local Motion.* The denial of their reduction to local motion should not be taken to mean that local motion does not play a role in the qualities of matter, for such motion appears to accompany all qualitative changes. All we want to say is that, contrary to the claim of mechanism, the qualities of matter do not consist in motion alone. In other words, it is not possible to explain these qualities

by means of local motion alone. This is the only point we wish to consider here, for the value of mechanism as a general philosophy of nature has already been considered in Chapter V. The proof of our assertion is as follows:

The principle of inertia, which states that a moving body continues to move in a uniform and rectilinear way unless acted upon by an outside force, philosophically requires a cause (*not* a force) explaining why this motion continues. As we have seen in no. 86, this cause is traditionally called impetus, but it may also be given the more modern name of kinetic energy. This impetus is not the body itself, for otherwise every body would necessarily have it and consequently would be in motion; for the same reason, it is not extension or the quantity of the body; it is not the force that made the body begin to move, for this force can attain the body only as long as it is in contact with this body; it is not the body's motion itself, for this motion is a being-moved and not an active moving. Consequently, it has to be a quality. This quality, which causes the continuation of the motion, arises from the external force that sets the body in motion and makes it possible also for the body to cause effects in other bodies. Therefore, locomotion does not make material qualities superfluous, for it itself presupposes a quality.

Moreover, if there were no qualities at all in the material world except locomotion, it would be impossible to perform quantitative measurements, so that experimental science would be impossible. Whenever we want to measure an object, determine its place or its motion, we have to sense in one way or another that this object stands out against its surroundings. For instance, a thermometer filled with a fully transparent liquid would be completely useless for measuring temperature because the level reached by· the liquid could not be read; a moving particle which would not leave any direct or indirect trace could not be observed. In other words, since pure quantity and pure motion, as such, are not observable, there can be no experimental science of matter without qualities.

132. *Metaphysical Nature of Material Qualities.* Concerning the mode of being pertaining to material qualities, it is to be noted that they do not exist separately but only in a subsistent material subject. Color, for instance, does not exist except as a modification of matter, and chemical properties do not float around all by themselves but inhere in a subject as affinities of this subject. Qualities, therefore, are what we have called in metaphysics predicamental accidents or secondary modes of being.[2]

From the logical point of view, some material qualities are properties, while others are predicable accidents. Qualities which flow from the essence of a material being are properties. They are of necessity connected with this essence and, therefore, will naturally exist in a being having the essence in question. For instance, if it is admitted that water is endowed with its own specific essence, then its specific gravity and boiling point may be considered as properties. On the other hand, qualities which do not flow of necessity from the essence of a material subject, but are found only in certain individuals, are predicable accidents. As such we may name the degree of heat possessed by water and the particular impetus imparted to a body through collision with another body.

2. QUALITY AND QUANTITY

133. Although quantity and quality are distinct secondary modes of being, they are not unrelated as they concretely exist in nature. In several ways a quality may be be said to be quantified.

Indirect Quantification of a Quality. First of all, both quantity and quality may be accidents of one and the same

---

[2]Cf. the author's *Metaphysics,* nos. 208 ff.

subsistent subject or material substance. This substance or body is spatially dispersed by its quantity and, consequently, a material quality pertaining to the body will also be spatially dispersed, i.e., extended or quantified. Technically this quantification is a kind of *indirect* quantity because the quality is affected by the quantity of its subject. In this sense a quality may increase or decrease in extension according as its subject becomes bigger or smaller. For instance, there is more redness in a rose when its size increases. However, this kind of quantification merely refers to the extension of the subject having the color; the expanse affected by the color is greater, but the color itself does not become more intense.

In connection with this indirect quantity, it may be useful to point out that a quality may be quantified not only because of its spatial extension but also because of its temporal aspect. In other words, in addition to the fixed continuity of spatial extension, a quality may also have the fluid continuity that characterizes its material subject. This quantification affects a quality in the same way as it affects the subject of the quality in question; hence we may speak, for instance, of the topological and metric structure of a quality. "John became scarlet at 10:00 A.M." refers to the topological temporal structure of his color, while "He blushed for ten minutes" indicates its metric structure.

Secondly, the quality of a body may have a quantitative aspect insofar as it is able to produce an *extended effect* in another object. Saccharin, for instance, may be called much sweeter than sugar because it leads to the perception of a sweet flavor over a greater area of the tongue than an equal amount of ordinary sugar. This quantification of the quality "sweetness" is still *indirect,* for it is determined by the extension of the organ affected by the quality.

Thirdly, we may speak of the indirect quantity of a quality insofar as the intensity of its *effect* is considered.

To use the same example, saccharin not only acts on more taste buds but also leads to a more intense sensation of sweetness. The quantification of a quality by the intensity of its effect is still indirect, for it directly refers to the quantity of something extrinsic to the quality in question.

134. *Direct Quantification of a Quality.* A quality may also be quantified in a direct way—namely, in the sense that a subject participates in a greater or lesser degree in a qualitative perfection. For instance, a powerful magnet has the quality of magnetism to a higher degree than a weak magnet.

There is an evident connection between this direct quantity of a quality and its indirect quantification through its effects. By virtue of the metaphysical principle that action follows being,[3] an agent has to be more perfect if it produces more perfect effects. Moreover, we do not have any direct insight into the nature of a being but know this nature only through the operations whose principle it is. Consequently, we can judge the quality of a being only by means of the effects it produces.

Analogous Use of the Term "Quantity." It should be noted that this direct quantification of qualities is not limited to the realm of matter. Even in the case of strictly spiritual qualities we are entitled to speak about quantity in this sense. For instance, it is meaningful to say that Peter is *more* intelligent or *more* strong-willed than John. Quantitative terms are used even with respect to essential perfections; e. g., man is essentially *more* perfect than a plant.

In such uses of quantitative terms there is no longer question of quantity in the univocal sense in which they apply to the spatial and temporal dispersion of a body, but merely of analogous applications. With respect to spiritual qualities and essential characteristics one cannot

---

[3] Cf. the author's *Metaphysics*, no. 245.

speak of spatial or temporal dispersion in the same sense as the term applies to extended bodies. Even when a quantitative term is used in reference to the intensity of a quality or of its effects, there is only an analogous application of that term. A simple example may make this point clear. In a univocal use of quantitative terms we may add one quantity to another to obtain twice the original. For instance, 212 apples plus 212 apples give us a total of 424 apples. But if I add boiling water to boiling water, I do not get a temperature of 424°F. In other words, the measurement of intensity differs from that of extended quantity, because intensity differs from extension. Although both are measurable because of their quantitative aspects, intensity and extension are not of the same nature. Consequently, the quantity of intension merely is analogous to that of extension.

On the other hand, when we speak about the indirect quantity of a quality insofar as we consider its extension over a certain spatial area, there is question of quantity in the primary sense of the term. By blowing up a balloon and thereby increasing its surface by 100 square inches, we also increase at the same time and in the same sense the area over which its color extends.

135. *Measurement of Qualities.* The fact that qualities are quantified makes it possible to measure them and to investigate them by means of mathematical methods. With respect to the *extension* of a quality, this possibility should be obvious, for it is merely a question of measuring the extension of the body whose quality it is. Because different parts of a body may have different qualities or at least the same quality in a different degree of intensity, the resulting qualitative heterogeneity may be charted and submitted to the appropriate mathematical analysis.

Regarding the direct quantity or *intensity* of qualities, here, too, measurement is possible. For the qualities can be arranged at least[4] in the order of their increasing or decreasing intensity. This is sufficient to justify the use of a mathematical method.

The possibility of applying mathematical methods to material qualities does not imply that these qualities have been wholly reduced to quantity. All that is prerequisite for the application of a mathematical method is that the qualities under consideration have some quantitative aspect, at least in an analogous sense. As was explained above, this condition is fulfilled by material qualities not only because of their extension but also because of their intensity.

136. *The Metaphysical Foundation for the Interrelationship of Quantity and Quality.* A first metaphysical basis for the relationship of quantity and quality may be sought in the fact that both are accidental modes of being pertaining to one and the same material substance. Because quantity extends this substance spatially (and temporally), the material substance is not wholly and entirely in just one point and, consequently, any material quality of this substance will necessarily have to be extended also. Reversely, qualities determine a material being as it concretely exists, i.e., as quantified by its spatial and temporal dispersion. Consequently, quantity itself is qualified by the qualities of the extended subject.

A more profound explanation may be given by a consideration of the fundamental non-simplicity of material substances. As we have seen in Chapter III, a body is essentially composed of matter and form as its constituent principles. Form plays the role of the determining or active principle, and matter that of the determinable or

---

[4]We say "at least" because there is another possibility of measurement. If an intensity varies in a continuous way, there is a value that lies exactly midway between two given intensities; hence there is a possibility of expressing the proportions of intensities as equal or unequal. Cf. P. Hoenen, *Cosmologia,* no. 140.

passive principle. This composite character proper to the very nature of material being has a counterpart in the accidental order. Qualities distinguish and determine the subject and, by distinguishing and determining it, they also render its quantity distinguished and determined in the same way. This determination of quantity by quality has a certain similarity to that of matter by form. Quantity, on the other hand, by dispersing the body prevents it from having its qualities in an indivisible way. Thus the dispersion of the material substance by quantity implies that the qualities of this substance will be likewise dispersed. But dispersion means divisibility and openness to the influence of other quantified beings, both of which are signs of the passivity and determinability that is characteristic of matter. For this reason we may say that quantity and quality have an interrelationship resembling that of matter and form.

3. QUALITATIVE CHANGE OR ALTERATION

137. *Meaning and Kinds of Alterations.* In a broad sense the term alteration is used for any kind of accidental change. In a strict sense, as we want to use it here, it means a modification of a quality.

Two general types of alterations may be distinguished. First, the change by which a subject acquires a quality which previously it did not have or loses one it did have. Such changes may accompany a substantial change of the subject or occur without any substantial change. For instance, if water is considered to be essentially different from hydrogen and oxygen, then the substantial change by which these two gases are combined into water is accompanied by the appearance of a new set of specific qualities, such as specific gravity, boiling point, etc. On the other hand, if a body is given an impetus through collision, it acquires a quality without becoming essentially different.

Secondly, an alteration may consist in a diminution or increase of intensity of an existing quality. An example would be the rise or fall of the temperature of a steel beam from fifty to one hundred degrees or vice versa.

The problems regarding alteration which we want to consider here are the following: 1) What is the origin of new specific qualities or the relationship between alteration and substantial change? 2) What is the nature of increase or decrease of intensity?

138. *The Origin of New Specific Qualities.* Specific qualities are properties flowing of necessity from the essence of a being. For this reason we may say that new specific qualities are secondary effects of the essential change that gives rise to a new substance. The efficient cause which induces the essential change causes a new substantial form to actuate matter and, because of the necessary connection between this form and the new properties, it causes also these properties.

The point, however, we want to investigate here is whether there is any ontological relationship between the new set of properties and the former specific qualities that were present before the substantial change. This question may be expressed in a different way—namely, can the efficient cause producing the essential change arbitrarily determine what kind of properties will exist in the new substance or are there any limitations imposed on its action by virtue of the properties existing in the body prior to the change?

With respect to the limitations governing substantial change, we may distinguish three fundamental reasons, which may be called formal, efficient, and material. *Formal* limitation arises from the fact that certain qualities are

152

specifically proper to each kind of substance; consequently, the efficient cause cannot produce one kind of substance and give it a set of properties pertaining to a different kind. For instance, the cause cannot produce sulfuric acid and give it the properties of water. This limitation, however, does not arise from the old properties of the subject that is changed, but from the necessary relationship between the new substantial form and its specific qualities. For this reason we call it a formal limitation.

Secondly, there is an *efficient* limitation. As experience shows, a material object may change more readily into one kind of matter than into another. Water, for example, is more easily changed into hydrogen and oxygen than into gold. Consequently, a different kind of efficient cause will be needed for the second change than for the first. In this way we may say that the nature of the efficient cause imposes a limitation on the kind of essential change it can produce and, consequently, also on the kind of properties it will give rise to in the new substance. Again, however, this limitation does not immediately arise from the old properties of the subject but from the nature of the efficient cause acting on it.

Thirdly, there is a kind of *material* limitation. It is closely connected with the preceding type. When an efficient cause[5] acts on a body, it is limited not only by the nature of the forces it possesses, but also by the fact that its action is exercised on a subject that concretely exists with this or that set of specific qualities. These qualities have definite ways of reacting to the influence exercised on them by the agent. What exactly these typical ways of reacting are can be determined only by experience. But observation shows that some qualities are more closely re-

---

[5]This assertion applies only to secondary efficient causes, not to the primary cause. For this distinction, see the author's *Metaphysics*, no. 249.

lated to those of one substance than those of another.[6] Consequently, it will be easier to change the material subject into one substance than into another because its present qualities predispose it more immediately for this change than for the other. Qualities as viewed in relation to substantial change are called material dispositions, and for this reason we call the limitation in question a *material* limitation.

Philosophically, the predisposition of a subject for certain changes in preference to others is expressed by saying that the subject is more immediately in potency to one change than to another. As far as the new qualities are concerned, we may say, therefore, that they pre-exist in the old substance in more or less immediate potency. The term "in more or less immediate potency" is used to distinguish their presence from actual and purely potential presence. Actual are the qualities here and now pertaining to the subject; purely potential are those that, absolutely speaking, can be actuated; in immediate potency are qualities which are close to becoming actual.

139. *Reduction of Qualities.* Through observation and experiments the physical sciences are able to determine what qualities will arise from the present properties of a given subject and thus reduce, for instance, the qualities of a compound to those of its elements by making intelligible why these and no others arise. Such a reduction does not mean that the new qualities are not essentially different from the old ones, no more than the relationship between a circle and an ellipse means that these two figures are essentially the same. All this reduction does is give a physical and more determined content to the philosophical expression that the new qualities pre-exist in immediate potency in the old properties.

---

[6]Again, the precise nature of the relationships between different qualities is something that has to be decided by experimental science.

Quality

140. *Decrease or Increase of Intensity of a Quality.*
Non-specific qualities, such as the heat and color of a body,
may be present in different degrees. By *intension* is meant
that a quality is changed from being present in a less
perfect state to being present in a more perfect state.
Remission means the opposite. Both intension and remission are kinds of alteration.

Intension does not consist in the corruption of the
existing quality and the generation of the same quality in
a higher degree. The situation here is not the same as
with respect to substantial forms. When a lower substantial form is replaced by a higher, e.g., that of non-
living matter by that of a plant, the material substratum is reduced to pure potency and from this potency
the higher form is educed under the influence of the agent.
The reason is that substantial forms cannot be more or
less present. The substantial form is the determinant
principle of the essence, and any modification of this form
implies an essential difference and not merely a different
degree of the same specific essence. Hence, such a form
either is present or not, but it cannot be present in a more
perfect or less perfect way. The same, however, does not
hold for qualities that can be remitted or intensified. If a
body, for instance, is given a higher degree of heat, its
temperature does not first have to go down to absolute
zero and then rise to the degree in question.

Secondly, the increase in intensity does not take place in
the same way as an increase in extended quantity. An
extended body is quantitatively increased by the simple
addition of new integral parts. But a quality does not have
any integral parts and therefore cannot be intensified in
this way. At most, it could be extended over a greater
area.

The intension and remission of a quality should be conceived as a greater or lesser participation of their subject

in the mode of being, expressed by the quality in question, under the influence of the stronger or weaker action of an efficient cause. From general metaphysical principles it should be clear that any accident is a participation of a subject in the mode of being expressed by this accident.[7] If then, some accidents can be intensified or remitted, it follows that their mode of being can be participated in more or less perfectly by the subject.

4. QUALITIES AS ACTIVE POWERS

141. *Meaning of the Term.* By an active power we mean a principle by which a subject is capable of exercising influence on others. Such a principle may permanently reside in a material subject as a property flowing from its nature or be present only in a transitory way. Because material qualities exercise influence on others, they are principles of activity, either permanently or transitorily. An example of the first is chemical affinity and of the second the instrumental power of a saw in the hands of a carpenter.

The activity of such powers has its terminus in a subject distinct from the acting power and, therefore, is called a potency for transient action. The opposite of transient action is immanent action, i.e., action which remains in the operating potency as its perfection. Immanent action is found only in living beings.

Transient Action is in the Recipient. It is to be noted that the perfection of transient action is in the recipient, i.e., the subject on which the agent exercises its action, for the agent makes this subject be in-act with respect to the perfection in question. For instance, if one body heats another, this other obtains the perfection of being hot in-act or actually hot. The influence of the agent (the first body) produces in the recipient (the second body)

---

[7] Cf. the author's *Metaphysics,* no. 183.

a perfection (a certain degree of heat), which first was only in the agent. For this reason transient action is said to be in the recipient. However, this statement should not be understood as if the recipient were exercising the action in question. All it means is that the agent makes the recipient participate in a new perfection, so that this perfection exists now also in the recipient.

142. *Real Distinction of Active Power and Body.* In metaphysics we noted that there is a certain multiplicity of the finite individual being in the order of activity.[8] Remaining the same individual, the finite being can act and not act. This characteristic of finite being led us to the conclusion that in such a being nature and action are really distinct.

At present, however, a further investigation has to be made. The metaphysical thesis outlined above justified our conclusion that a finite being is in potency to action before it acts. What we want to investigate now is whether this potency to action is to be identified with the nature of the material substance or really distinct from it.[9] If there is a real distinction between the two, then the power to act is an accidental determination of this nature which, because it formally modifies the subject in itself, should be classified as a quality.

The following reason leads us to assert that the active powers of a body are not really identical with its nature. Whatever perfections are found in a subject have their intrinsic source either in its substantial form or in accidental forms.[10] For prime matter does not confer any perfection on a being but merely limits its perfection. Now the sub-

---

[8]Cf. the author's *Metaphysics*, nos. 182 ff.

[9]We are concerned here only with material beings or bodies and their active powers. However, the line of thought presented here applies also to the powers of non-material beings.

[10]The extrinsic source is the agent which caused the subject or its accidental modification.

stantial form cannot be an immediate principle of operation or operative potency. Therefore, operative potencies are really distinct from the nature of a material being.

The assertion that the substantial form cannot be an immediate[11] principle of activity may be proved in two ways.

1. By its very nature a substantial form is in-act, for its essential function is to actuate matter. If, then, the operative potency were really identical with the substantial form, this potency, too, would have to be in-act by its very nature and, therefore, always operating. But experience shows that the active powers of a body do not always operate. For instance, acid does not always corrode iron, but only when it is in contact with iron. Therefore, the operative potency cannot be really identical with the substantial form of a body.

2. A potency and its act must belong to the same general class, for they have to be proportionate to each other. The assertion that, for instance, the act of thinking proceeds from man's power of growth as its immediate principle would be unintelligible. But the substantial form of a body belongs to the genus of substance, while material action is an accident. Consequently, the substantial form cannot be really identical with the active power of a body.[12]

*HISTORICAL NOTES

143. As was already pointed out, *Locke* (1632-1704) denied the objectivity of secondary sense qualities. *Berkeley* (1685-1743) went a step farther and asserted the same of the primary qualities.

---

[11]The substantial form may be called an incomplete and remote principle of operation. Cf. the author's *Animate Nature,* no. 46.

[12]Certain difficulties can be raised against the real distinction of nature and active power. They can be solved in the same way as those that are put forward against the distinction of soul and operative potency. Cf. the author's *Animate Nature,* no. 43.

Rigid mechanism, represented by *Democritus* (born about 460 B. C.) and *Descartes* (1596-1650), attempted to explain all natural phenomena by means of locomotion alone and, consequently, denied all qualities and alterations. More moderate mechanists admit at least the quality of impetus.

Aristotle, Thomas Aquinas and most medieval philosophers further specified their doctrine of qualities by means of an antiquated physical theory of four fundamental qualities (hot, cold, wet, dry) and thus attempted to explain the phenomena of nature.

The possibility of applying mathematical methods to qualities was realized by philosophers living before experimental science became autonomous, but little or no progress was made in this direction prior to *Descartes*.

SUMMARY

144. A quality, in the strict sense, means an accident which formally modifies a substance in itself. A material quality may be sense-perceptible either immediately, such as color and sound, or only in its effects, e.g., chemical affinity. Proper or secondary sense qualities are perceived by only one sense, while common or primary sense qualities are perceived by more than one.

Even the proper sense qualities are real. Man is not aware of producing them through his consciousness, and they cannot be produced by his sense organs alone, for otherwise there would be no reason why different sense objects give rise to different perceptions of sense qualities. Consequently, there must be something in reality outside consciousness and outside the sense organs which gives rise to these perceptions. Hence the sense qualities are real, whatever their exact nature may be.

Although local motion plays an important role in material qualities, we cannot reduce them simply to such motion. For even local motion itself requires a cause (not a force) for its continuation; this cause is not the motion itself, for the local motion of a body is a being-moved; it is not the body or its quantity, for otherwise every body would of necessity be in motion; it is not the force which gave rise to the motion, for this force can attain the body only as long as it is in contact with it; consequently, it is a quality. Moreover, local motion without qualities would not be perceptible, so that quantitative measurements would be impossible. No experimental science of matter would be possible if there were no qualities which make different parts of matter distinguishable.

Material qualities do not exist separately but only as modifications of a subsistent subject or body. They are accidents in the predicamental sense of the term. From the logical point of view, some qualities are properties because they flow from the essence of the body in question, while others are predicable accidents because they are found only in certain individuals having the essence.

Quantity and quality are intimately related in material beings, although they are distinct modes of being. Both are accidents of one and the same material subject. The spatial and temporal dispersion of this subject by quantity indirectly disperses also its material qualities in space and time. A quality is quantified also because of the extended or intense character of the effect it produces. This quantification is still indirect, because it is derived from something extrinsic to the quality itself.

A quality is directly quantified insofar as a subject participates to a greater or lesser degree in a qualitative perfection. This quantification is connected as cause to effect with the intensity of the effect produced by the quality. It is to be noted, however, that the term "quantity" is used in an analogous sense when we speak of the direct quantity of a quality. There is no question of spatial or temporal dispersion, as such; hence the methods of measurement will differ from those of extended quantity.

The extension of a quality is measurable by the same methods as the extension of the body whose quality it is. Because of this extension the qualitative heterogeneity of a body can be charted and mathematically analysed. The intensity of a quality is subject to measurement at least because various intensities can be arranged in the order of their increase and decrease. By assigning numbers to the intensities, it becomes possible to use a mathematical method. The possibility of measuring qualities by quantity does not mean that qualities can be reduced to quantity, but merely that they possess some quantitative aspect.

The immediate metaphysical foundation for the relationship between quantity and quality lies in the fact that both are accidents of the same subject: quantity extends the qualified subject, and quality formally modifies the quantified subject. A more profound explanation may be sought in the hylomorphic composition of material beings insofar as this composition has a counterpart in the accidental order. Just as matter limits form and form determines matter, so quantity limits quality (by dispersing it in space and time) and quality determines quantity by giving it a certain characteristic. Matter makes the composite subject to dissolution, and quantity does the same for quality by extending it and thus exposing it to the influence of other quantified beings.

Alteration, in the strict sense, means either a change by which a quality is generated or corrupted or a change by which the intensity of a quality is modified.

New specific qualities are secondary effects of substantial change; therefore, their efficient cause is the agent producing the new substance. However, this agent is limited not only formally (by the necessary relationship of substantial form and certain properties) and efficiently (by the limitation of its own powers), but also materially, insofar as the specific properties of the old substance react in a typical way and therefore render the substance more immediately disposed to a change into a substance with related properties than into another with unrelated properties. In other words, certain properties may be said to pre-exist in immediate potency, while others are purely potential. It is the task of experimental science to determine concretely which properties may be said to pre-exist in this way by showing how certain properties can be reduced to others.

A change in intensity of a quality does not mean that the existing quality is corrupted and the same quality subsequently regenerated in a higher degree. Unlike a substantial form which either is present or absent, a qualitative form can be present more or less intensely. This change in intensity means that, under the influence of an external agent, a subject participates more or less in the mode of being represented by the quality in question.

Material qualities are principles or powers through which a body can act on other bodies. These active powers are really distinct from the matter-form nature of the material being. Matter is not a principle of any activity. The substantial form cannot be really identical with the operative principles, for otherwise these principles would have to be always acting because the substantial form is essentially act. Moreover, action is an accident and, therefore, requires an immediate principle in the accidental order. But the substantial form pertains to the genus of substance.

SUGGESTED READINGS

145.   Aristotle, *Physica,* bk. VII, chs. 1-4.

John Locke, *An Essay Concerning Human Understanding,* bk. II, ch. 8 (Fraser ed., 1894, vol. I, pp. 169-182).

Quality

Henry J. Koren, *Readings in the Philosophy of Nature:*

René Descartes, *Philosophical Principles of Nature,* pp. 111 ff.

Peter Hoenen, *The Measurement of Corporeal Qualities,* pp. 223 ff.

Fernand Van Steenberghen, *Epistemology,* New York, 1949, pp. 212-233.

Andrew G. van Melsen, *The Philosophy of Nature,* ch. VI.

Peter Hoenen, *Cosmologia,* Notae XI and XII.

CHAPTER TWELVE

CAUSALITY IN MATERIAL BEINGS

In the preceding pages the activity of material beings has been considered several times. We mentioned it in the question of dynamism when the possibility of action at a distance was discussed (no. 31), in our consideration of motion and the law of inertia (no. 86), and also in Chapter XI when we spoke of material qualities as principles of activity (nos. 141 f.). Material activity is nothing but another name for the exercise of causality by bodily beings.

The general study of causality pertains to the metaphysics of finite being.[1] The purpose of the present chapter is more limited. After briefly pointing out the relativity and analogous nature of causality in the material being, it aims at an investigation of the difficulties said to arise from the experimental study of matter with respect to the fundamental principles of causality, which are established in metaphysics by a consideration of the nature of finite being. Moreover, because formal and material causality have already been studied in chapters concerned with hylomorphism, we may restrict ourselves here to efficient and final causality.

Efficient Causality

146. *Relativity and Analogy of "Efficient Cause."* The theoretical distinction between cause and effect does not perfectly correspond to a distinction between beings in the sense that we can say that *A* is only the cause of *B,* and *B* only the effect of *A.* Every action of a material being

---

[1]Cf. the author's *Metaphysics,* Chs. XII ff.

on another object gives rise to a corresponding reaction, so that in one respect A is the cause of B but in another B is the cause of A. It merely depends on the viewpoint which one of two interacting bodies will be called cause and which one effect. We may say, for instance, that the stove causes the room to become hotter, but we could say also that the room causes the stove to become colder. In this sense cause and effect, as predicated of material beings, are *relative,* for the various parts of the universe constantly interact and therefore are both cause and effect in different respects. This relativity, however, does not mean that one may arbitrarily ascribe any causal action to any material being; for instance, we cannot say that the burning stove cools the room and that the room heats the stove.

Secondly, the term "efficient cause" does not apply in a univocal sense to all efficient causes but only *analogously.* Man's idea of causality is derived, first of all, from the observation of specifically human actions on material things, such as those manifested in the artifacts produced by a craftsman. These products reveal the superiority and originality of their maker—superiority or independence because their maker is not changed by them to the same extent as a hot stove is cooled by its surroundings, originality because the human cause is capable of producing highly diversified effects in contrast to the limited possibilities open to purely material agents, such as a stove. The causality of such agents is characterized by reciprocity, dependence, and lack of originality. They are acted upon as much as they act, their action is wholly a reaction and is determined by their own nature and surroundings. Accordingly, although we may call material beings causes, their mode of being a cause differs from that of man, so that they are causes only in an analogous sense.

147. *The Philosophical Principle of Efficient Causality.* By a cause is meant an ontological principle which exercises

positive influence on the "to be", the coming to be, or the mode of being of something else.[2] The efficient cause is the external agent whose action produces the "to be", the coming to be, or the mode of being in question. As was explained in metaphysics,[3] such a cause is necessary for every being which does not have within itself a sufficient reason for its "to be." This truth is expressed in the so-called principle of (efficient) causality: every contingent being has a cause.

There would be no reason to consider this principle specifically in reference to the material world if it were not for certain problems that arise in connection with modern science. Although, as we have seen in Chapter One, in principle science and philosophy cannot contradict each other, the same cannot be asserted with respect to scientists and philosophers. In the present question conflicts have arisen mainly from two sources—namely, the spontaneous distintegration of radioactive atoms and more still from the so-called principle of uncertainty.

a. Efficient Causality and Spontaneous Disintegration

148. In radioactive materials atoms may suddenly disintegrate in such a way that the scientist is unable to indicate any reason why the change comes about here and now. As far as observation goes, no cause can be assigned to the phenomenon. In a similar way, an electron may suddenly jump from a higher to a lower energy level, again without there being any observable cause. This puzzling situation is sometimes expressed by saying that these phenomena do not have a cause.

Ambiguity of the Term "Cause." Before criticizing this expression, it may be useful to point out that the term "cause" often does not have exactly the same meaning in

---

[2]Cf. *op. cit.*, nos. 228 ff.
[3]Cf. *op. cit.*, chs. XII and XIII.

philosophy and in science. We have already indicated in what sense "cause" is understood in traditional philosophy. Science, on the other hand, speaks of a cause when an observable antecedent is regularly followed by a consequent phenomenon in such a way that there is a dependence of the consequent on the antecedent or at least a constant functional relationship. Moreover, it often narrows down the use of the term to mechanical functions. These uses differ considerably from the philosophical meaning of the term, even if we restrict ourselves to the efficient cause. For they apply only to an observable interconnection and this connection is further limited to the realm of mechanical phenomena, or even reduced to a purely functional relationship[4] which may or may not be causal in the philosophical sense.

149. *Phenomena Without a Cause.* With respect to the above-mentioned "causeless" phenomena, the meaning of the expression may be limited to the level on which verification by the senses is possible. Taken in this sense, there is no reason to object to it. All it means then is that no observable antecedent phenomenon has yet been discovered by which the subsequent disintegration or "jump" to another energy level can be explained.

However, the expression is dangerous, for it could easily be taken to mean that the phenomenon in question does not have a cause in the philosophical sense of the term. If this sense is intended, then the expression would be against the metaphysical principle of efficient causality, for it would imply that there is a contingent being without a sufficient reason for its "to be." This second sense is not based on the results of science, but on the gratuitous metaphysical

---

[4]A relationship is purely functional when the mathematical value of one magnitude depends on that of another. Such a relationship does not purport to state anything about the ontological connection of the realities—if any—represented by the magnitudes in question.

principle of positivism that only the observable is real or meaningful, so that philosophical causality is devoid of importance. In practice, no scientist accepts the absence of a cause in the metaphysical sense, for the very purpose of his research is to find the reasons why material objects act as they do, i.e., the causes that are at work in matter.

b. Causality and Determinism

150. For a good understanding of the difficulties raised against the principle of causality from the viewpoint of twentieth century science, it is necessary to make here a few remarks about the development of science and the new world picture offered by contemporary scientists.

The Transformation of the Principle of Causality. If we limit our considerations to the material world in which we live, the principle of causality may be expressed also in this way: every phenomenon is fully determined by its causes (i.e., its mode of being as well as its coming-to-be depend on these causes). As far as this principle is concerned, it makes no difference whether these causes are free or act of necessity. However, a cause that acts of necessity, itself is determined, for it has no possibility of acting or not-acting or of choosing between different courses of action. By its very nature such a cause is necessitated to act and, in the concrete conditions surrounding it, its way of acting is rigorously fixed once and for all by an intrinsic necessity. Because the question of free-will activity does not arise in a purely material world, the interaction of purely material processes cannot take any other course than the one determined by their respective natures. For this reason such processes are said to be deterministic: if A happens, then B will happen of necessity.

Mechanical processes, i.e., processes running their course through local motion and impact, most strikingly reveal their deterministic nature. In the evolution of scientific thought mechanical operations played a predominant role, so that scientists readily identified deterministic causality with mechanical causality. It is to be noted, however, that there is no *a priori* reason why deterministic causes would necessarily have to be mechanical. Experience alone can determine whether this identification is justifiable.

Flushed by the success of their mechanical explanations, scientists of the preceding centuries did not hesitate to consider the whole universe as nothing but one enormously complex machine. Every part of it was supposed to act in a fully determined mechanistic way by virtue of iron-clad laws allowing no interference and no exceptions. As a consequence of this world view they rejected man's free-will actions, for they would have interfered with this mechanical universe.[5] In this way physical determinism becomes mechanical determinism.

The mechanistic position entailed as a further consequence that any mind powerful enough to understand all laws of nature and to know the exact condition of the universe at any given moment would be able to predict with absolute accuracy everything that will happen in the future as well as calculate everything that has happened in the past, in much the same way as astronomers are able to calculate past and future eclipses of the sun (Laplace's "demon"). Of course, it was realized that man could not, or at least not yet, lay claim to such knowledge. Nevertheless this knowledge was the ideal to be pursued and—who knows—perhaps to be attained at a future date. This consequence of mechanistic determinism was laid down in the assertion: when the present condition of an isolated system is known in all its determinant factors, its future conditions can be calculated from it (the principle of predictability). In this way the philosophical principle of

---

[5]For the solution of the difficulties that can be raised against free will from the viewpoint of physical determinism, see the author's *Animate Nature*, no. 149.

causality was progressively transformed into a principle governing the activity of necessary causes, the activity of mechanical causes and, finally, into a principle about the possibility of predicting the activity of these mechanical causes.

151. *The Crisis of this World-View.* Even the scientists of the nineteenth century knew that the inaccuracies inherent in human observation precluded absolutely exact knowledge of a system in all its details. First of all, man's senses limit the exactness of his observation as soon as he is concerned with the microscopic world. Secondly, any instrument used in measurements disturbs the situation to be observed. For instance, a thermometer dropped into a tank of water to determine its temperature, changes this temperature, so that it does not exactly indicate how hot the water was without the thermometer. Thirdly, a phenomenon may be so complex that it defies accurate information about all its factors and allows only a statistical average. For example, the exact position and velocity of individual particles of gas in a container escapes us, but we can measure the average frequency with which they will collide with the walls of the container and thus arrive at a mechanical explanation of the pressure.

However, these limitations of accuracy did not seem seriously to endanger the aspirations of nineteenth century science. The limitations imposed on observation by our sense organs applied equally to that of the predicted future state of the system; the disturbance caused by instruments could be calculated with reasonable accuracy; and the impossibility of determining the individual velocity and position of gas molecules was held to be merely of a practical nature. Thus scientists retained full confidence in the fundamental truth of their view.

This confidence, however, was wrecked by the discovery of the sub-atomic world. Experience shows that this world cannot be adequately described in mechanical terms, such as position and velocity of particles. The more determined the position is attributed to a particle, the less a definite velocity can be ascribed to it, and vice versa (Heisenberg's principle of uncertainty or indeterminism). Consequently, it is in principle impossible ever to obtain accurate knowledge of the conditions governing the future action of such particles. Therefore, it is in principle impossible to predict the future states of a system consisting of such particles.

In this way it became clear that the mechanical world picture of the nineteenth century had to be abandoned. The necessity of modifying this picture is often expressed in these words: twentieth century science has definitely shown that the principle of causality is not valid.

152. *The Validity of the Principle of Causality.* In the light of the preceding pages it should not be difficult to understand what the claims of scientists really mean: we have to abandon the nineteenth century ideal of accurate prediction. If the exact predictability of future events from the initial conditions of a system is called a *physical* principle of causality, we may fully grant the claim of modern scientists that this principle is no longer valid. On the other hand, if their conclusions are supposed to mean that the *philosophical* principle of causality is no longer valid, then we cannot accept this claim. The philosophical principle simply states that every contingent being has a cause and says absolutely nothing about the possibility of predicting the activity of causes. Consequently, it is not affected in any way by the shifting positions of scientists with respect to this possibility.

153. *The Validity of Determinism.* We may even go further and claim that the results of science do not prove anything against the necessary or deterministic nature of

material causality. All science shows is that the *mechanical* conception of determinism is no longer tenable. But, as we pointed out above, there is no *a priori* reason why determinism should be conceived in a mechanical way, so that experience has to decide whether or not the mechanical view of material causality should be admitted. If, then, science shows that *mechanical* determinism cannot be held, it would be an illegitimate procedure to conclude that there is no determinism at all, unless positive proofs are offered for indeterminism in the philosophical sense of the term.

Such proofs, however, are lacking. The reason is that the laws of science themselves would become meaningless if there were no determinism in the philosophical sense of this term. The laws we have in mind here are precisely the statistical laws about the behavior of particles. Although it is not possible to know accurately what every individual particle will do, there are laws which formulate the probable frequency with which a certain type of action will occur. An example is the disintegration law which determines the "half-life" of radium as 1600 years, i.e., half of the atoms will have disintegrated after 1600 years. Such a law expresses nothing at all about the individual atoms of radium, but indicates what half of them will do within the specified time. The law would be meaningless if the disintegration of the individual particles were fully undetermined, for in that case complete chaos would prevail. There would be no reason why, for instance, only half of the atoms would disintegrate in 1600 years. It could just as well happen that none would disintegrate for a thousand years and then all at the same moment. If nothing determines the moment of disintegration of the individuals then there is nothing on which the statistical laws can be based. Therefore, we may say that these laws themselves presuppose the validity of philosophical determinism.

We may approach the validity of philosophical determinism also in this way:

A *priori,* there are three possibilities for explaining the action (disintegration) of a particle:

1. The action occurs without being determined by a cause.

2. The action is determined by a cause which acts of its own free choice.

3. The action is determined by a cause which acts of necessity.

The first possibility cannot be accepted, for it would be against the metaphysical principle of causality. Such an action would be a contingent being without a sufficient reason for its being.

The second is not acceptable, for free choice refers to an attribute of man or higher beings. Although scientists sometimes use the term "free choice" in speaking about the behavior of individual particles, no one seriously wants to assert that there is really question of freedom in the sense in which the term applies to human acts of will.

This leaves only the third possibility, in which the action in question follows of necessity from the nature of the non-free cause. It is true, of course, that the exact nature of this necessity escapes us. We know now that it is not mechanical, but are unable to state positively how it works.

If, despite the validity of these arguments for the determination of nature, many scientists persist in denying it, the reason must be sought outside science—namely in the positivistic philosophical view that only the observable is meaningful, and that the metaphysical necessity of determinism in non-free causes is nothing but "important nonsense." Evidently, such a view is no longer a consequence flowing from science, but is itself a metaphysical thesis.

Its validity or lack of it has to be determined by a critique of the philosophical arguments offered in its support.[6]

2. FINAL CAUSALITY

154. *The Principle of Finality.* As was explained in general metaphysics,[7] the final cause is that for the sake of which something is done or the end intended by the action of the agent.[8] Every agent acts for an end either because he himself directs his activity to the end he intends or, if the agent is not endowed with an intellect, because the action of the agent is directed to an end by the very nature of the agent. The statement that every agent acts for an end is called the principle of finality.[9]

The validity of the principle of finality in the realm of matter is sometimes assailed on the ground that efficient causality or the forces of matter alone are sufficient to explain the processes of nature. Hence final causality would be a superfluous feature, introduced merely because of an anthropological view of matter or because certain efficient factors in nature are left out of consideration.

---

[6]It would lead us too far afield to present this critique here. The reader may be referred, e.g., to P. Henry van Laer, *Philosophico-Scientific Problems*, Pittsburgh, 1954, ch. 3, pp. 28-58, or C. E. M. Joad, *A Critique of Positivism*, Chicago, 1950, ch. IV, pp. 43-62, Frederick Copleston, *Contemporary Philosophy*, London, 1956, Chs. II-V.

[7]Cf. the author's *Metaphysics*, ch. 14.

[8]We may leave out of consideration here the so-called *end of the agent* as opposed to the end of the *action*.

[9]The truth of the principle of finality may be made clear in this way. If the agent did not act for a definite end, i.e., for this effect rather than that, the agent would be indifferent or undetermined with respect to its possible effects. But what is undetermined to this effect cannot be the sufficient reason why this follows rather than that. Consequently, it could not be the efficient cause of this effect, for otherwise this effect would not have a sufficient reason for being. The same can be asserted of any effect assignable to the agent. Therefore, an agent which does not act for an end does not produce any effect, so that it is not an agent. Accordingly, if a being is an agent, it acts for an end. Cf. St. Thomas, *Contra Gentes*, bk. 3, ch. 2.

A Misconception. In reply, we may point out that a misconception of final causality underlies this objection. The final cause is not a supplement added to the efficient causes to remedy their deficiency, as is sometimes asserted even by proponents of final causes, nor superimposed on these causes to correct them, as it were, from without. The final causality of a material agent should be conceived as the intrinsic tendency of a material being to act in such a way that a certain end is reached, unless its causality is interfered with by other agents.[10]

Or to say it differently, the causal process by which a new material situation arises can be described in two ways. We can look upon it from the viewpoint of its origin (efficient causality) or from the standpoint of its terminus (final causality). For instance, when a rock breaks loose from a mountain, its descent can be described as resulting from the force of gravitation combined with the forces of resistance exercised by the obstacles which it finds on its path. This is a description in terms of efficient causality.[11] But we may also say that the stone seeks to reach the place of the least potential energy with the minimum of work. In this case the event is described in terms of final causality. There is no question here of superimposing the action of a final cause on the efficient causes, but merely of looking at the same causal process from a different viewpoint.

------

[10]We leave out of consideration here the extrinsic final causality by which an intellect can coordinate the activities of material agents to reach a purpose transcending the inherent natural ends to which the action of these agents tend.

[11]It is to be noted that forces, such as gravitation, which are popularly described as attracting or pulling toward themselves are just as much efficient causes as those which drive or push. It would be a serious mistake to speak about gravitation as a final cause because it draws objects to the center of attraction. Pushing and pulling both belong to the same genus of causality—namely, that of efficient causes. If the final cause is sometimes said to attract, this term should be understood in an analogous sense, in the same way as the good is spoken of as attractive.

Likewise, inherent final causality does not imply that the action of the efficient causes is modified so as to reach an effect that otherwise would not be brought about. If the efficient cause acts in a deterministic way, as is the case with purely physical causes, then the final cause or end to which the efficient cause tends is also implied and determined of necessity by the nature of the efficient cause.

155. *The Necessity of Final Causality.* Reverting to the objection against final causes in matter, we may say that in principle any material process may be described in terms of efficient causality. This description, however, is not adequate because it leaves unanswered the question why the efficient cause produces this effect and not that one. The reply to this question lies in the admission of an inherent principle of orientation or final cause. This principle translates the determination of the agent's nature into a determination of the agent's activity with respect to the effect that is to follow from the action of the agent.

There would be question of an anthropomorphic view of final causality in material agents only if we were to assert that inherent final causality operates in the same way as man does in directing the forces of matter to a purpose of his choosing. Such a purpose would be superimposed on the material agents. But the inherent final causality of material agents is nothing but the causal process of their activity viewed from the standpoint of the end to which this activity tends by virtue of the nature proper to the material agent.

SUMMARY

156. The notion of efficient cause applies only in a relative way to purely material beings, for the action of these beings is always an interaction, so that what in one re-

spect is the cause of this being in another respect is its effect.

As compared with man's specifically human causality in the production of artifacts, purely material beings are efficient causes only in analogous sense. They lack the superiority and originality proper to man and their mode of being causes is characterized by reciprocity, dependence and determinism.

The philosophical principle of efficient causality states that every contingent being has a cause, because otherwise it would be without a sufficient reason for its being. Some expressions of modern scientists seem to indicate that this principle is no longer valid. However, the terminology of science and philosophy is no longer the same and this accounts for the difference. In philosophy we speak about an efficient cause when an external agent through its action makes something else come to be or to be different, while science, if it uses the term "cause," means an observable antecedent that is regularly followed by an observable consequent, dependent on the antecedent, or even merely functionally related to it. Thus when, e.g., the disintegration of an atom is said to be causeless, the meaning is that no observable antecedent has yet been discovered. The absence of such a cause has nothing to do with the philosophical principle of causality.

In relation to purely material phenomena the philosophical principle of causality may be formulated as: every phenomenon is fully determined by physical causes whose action is fully determined by their very nature. In the course of the preceding centuries this philosophical determinism was identified with mechanical determinism, and mechanical determinism became identified with the possibility of predicting the future states of the universe. When twentieth century science showed that this predictability was in principle impossible, scientists began to say that the principle of causality was no longer valid. This assertion may be granted if the causality in question is understood as predictability and the mechanical determinism of nature. But it cannot be accepted if there is question of the philosophical principle of causality or the philosophical determinism of necessary causes. The statistical laws themselves which have replaced mechanical laws presuppose philosophical determinism, for if nothing determines the events whose probability is laid down in statistical laws, then these laws have no foundation. Moreover, a philosophical insight teaches us that a necessary or non-free cause acts in a necessary or deterministic way, so that the determinism of nature is not invalidated by the rejection of mechanical determinism.

The principle of finality states that every agent acts for an end. The final cause does not supplement deficiencies of efficient causality or necessarily modify the actions of efficient causes, but is the intrinsic tendency of a material being to act in such a way that its effect is reached, unless its causality is interfered with by other agents. In other words, the causal process can be described in two ways: from the viewpoint of its origin (efficient cause) or from the standpoint of the terminus to be reached (final cause). The second viewpoint requires an inherent principle of orientation which translates the determinate nature of the agent into a determinate activity in view of the effect that is to follow from the action of the agent.

SUGGESTED READINGS

157. Henry J. Koren, *Readings in the Philosophy of Nature:*

Max Born, *Wave Mechanics and Its Statistical Interpretation* pp. 371 ff.

Max Plank, *The Concept of Causality in Physics,* pp. 377 ff.

P. Henry van Laer, *Causality, Determinism, Previsibility, and Modern Science,* pp. 388 ff.

Andrew G. van Melsen, *The Philosophy of Nature,* ch. 7 and ch. 5, no. 3.

P. Henry van Laer, *Philosophico-Scientific Problems,* ch. 6.

EPILOGUE

158. The preceding chapters were meant only as a brief introduction to the main problems the philosopher encounters in his study of the material world. Their primary purpose was to acquaint the student with these problems and their solution in the light of Aristotelian-Thomistic principles and to encourage his personal research. For this reason we did not hesitate to append suggested readings containing many works which take a radically different view from the replies presented in the text.

Summarizing briefly the results of our study, we first investigated whether there still is room for a philosophy of nature, and the relationship this philosophy has to the sciences of nature and metaphysics. We then devoted considerable time to a discussion of hylomorphism, taking particular care to point out how much attention must be paid to the analogous nature of metaphysical concepts if a satisfactory explanation is to be given to the matter-form composition of bodies.

After a brief consideration of the philosophical inadequacy present in dynamism, mechanism, and hylosystemism, we proceeded to examine the properties of matter, starting from quantity and its relation to bodily substance and ending with a discussion of causality in material beings. The analyses of traditional philosophy were presented and wherever they seemed to conflict with science we investigated the so-called consequences of physics.

159. We saw how modern science has rendered obsolete many of the physical views which former ages had attached to the metaphysical study of nature. But we noted also how the traditional philosophical positions, once they are stripped of their antiquated physical appendages for-

eign to their nature, can be successfully confronted with the data of science—provided that science likewise is stripped of implied philosophical assumptions that are not based on the data of experience.

The ability of the Aristotelian-Thomistic philosophy of nature to hold its ground without becoming an anachronism, despite the revolutionary advances of experimental science, should not surprise us. Two reasons may be given for it. First of all, the fundamental tenets of this philosophy are not based on the results of science but on experiential data which science itself presupposes. Secondly, in principle, theses of a genuinely metaphysical nature are not subject to verification by the senses, so that no amount of experimental research can ever dislodge them from their position.

At the same time, however—and in this respect the history of the past centuries teaches a very eloquent lesson—the philosopher of nature must be constantly on guard not to introduce in his speculation elements that are foreign to the character of philosophy or mistake habitual patterns of thought for genuine philosophical insights. For this reason he cannot retreat to the pinnacles of an ivory tower there to contemplate eternal and unchangeable truths in splendid isolation, but has to maintain contact with the scientist lest he fail in his quest of truth.

REVIEW QUESTIONS

CHAPTER ONE—INTRODUCTION

SECTION

tory stage of science, (b) petrified science, (c) a synthesis of the results of science, (d) a logical analysis of scientific propositions, (e) a philosophical analysis of scientific methods, or (f) a philosophical reflection on the results of science?

20   12. How do idealists (Hegel) and phenomenologists (Nicolai Hartmann) conceive the philosophy of nature?

20   13. How is this philosophy conceived by modern Aristotelian-Thomistic thinkers?

21   14. Distinguish between the critique of the sciences and philosophy of nature.

22   15. Indicate St. Thomas' distinction of three degrees of abstraction and the corresponding levels on which scientific knowledge can terminate.

23   16. What position is assigned to philosophy of nature by those who still retain this classical division?

CHAPTER TWO—THE STARTING POINT OF HYLOMORPHISM

28   1. What is meant by hylomorphism?

29–30   2. Indicate what is meant by the analogous character of the term "essence," prior to presenting a proof of hylomorphism from substantial change.

31   3. Is there any connection between the retention of hylomorphism for the inanimate world and the substantial unity of man?

32–33   4. Explain the analogy of the term "individual" prior to presenting a proof of hylomorphism from the multiplication of individuals in the same species.

34   5. What would you reply to the objection that the preceding proof cannot conclude to

183

CHAPTER FOUR—Hylomorphism and Some Data of Science

52   1. Does the discontinuity of matter militate against hylomorphism?

53   2. Why is the transformation of "matter" into energy irrelevant with respect to hylomorphism?

54   3. May prime matter be identified with the nucleus of an atom?

55   4. Reply to this objection: experience shows that atoms continue to exist in a compound molecule. Therefore, such a compound is not a substance in the philosophical sense of the term, but an aggregate.

56   5. Reply to this objection: large units of matter are never completely pure. Therefore, such units cannot have only one specific form, but are aggregates.

57   6. Can the whole universe, or at least the whole non-human universe, be considered as a single individual substance?

58   7. Must we consider as individual substances a) each particle of matter, b) each atom, c) each molecule of the non-living world?

58   8. Why is it impossible to draw the exact boundary line between aggregate and individual substance?

CHAPTER FIVE — Dynamism, Mechanism and Hylosystemism

61   1. State the principal tenets of dynamism.

62   2. Can dynamism explain extension?

63   3. Is matter purely active?

CHAPTER SIX—QUANTITY

Review Questions

SECTION

presupposes the possibility of an actually infinite number.

(c) A perfect sphere touches a perfect plane in only one point, yet by rolling over the plane it produces a line. Therefore, this extended line consists only of unextended points.

77   8. Why should fields of forces be considered as extended?

CHAPTER SEVEN—MOTION

81   1. Define motion and show by an analysis of motion that this definition is justified.

81   2. Why do we say that what is in motion was moving in the past and will be moving in the future?

82   3. In what sense is motion an imperfect act?

82   4. Why is motion irreducible to any static act?

83   5. How can we say that motion is real since its past no longer exists, its future is not yet, and its past and future are separated only by an indivisible point?

84   6. Reply to Zeno's objections to motion: (a) in moving, an object would have to pass through an infinite number of points, which is impossible. (b) The tortoise could never be overtaken by Achilles if the animal is given a small handicap, because Achilles would have to travel through an infinite number of short distances before he can catch up with the tortoise. (c) At every moment of time an arrow does not move; therefore, it does not move in the whole of time.

85   7. What gives motion its unity? From what does this principle of unity arise?

187

Review Questions

CHAPTER NINE—Space

SECTION		
99	1.	What is meant by absolute space?
100	2.	Is absolute space a real or a logical being?
100	3.	Is absolute space a purely logical being?
*101–103	4.	Are real beings and space of less or more than three dimensions metaphysically impossible?
*104	*5.	What is meant by "curved space"? Is such space metaphysically impossible?

CHAPTER TEN—Time

108	1.	Describe what is meant by time and explain the description.
109	2.	Indicate the analogies of place (space) and time.
110	3.	What is the relation between time and motion?
110	4.	What motion is generally used for measuring time and why?
111	5.	Distinguish the three types of duration called eternity, eviternity, and time.
112	6.	What is absolute time? Is it a real or a logical being?
113	7.	What is so-called "real" time? Is it a real or a logical being?
113	8.	How can we say that time is real since its numbering takes place in the mind?
113	9.	How can we claim that "real" time exists outside the mind since its past and future parts are not now?
114	10.	What is meant by the classical principle of relativity?

189

CHAPTER ELEVEN—QUALITY

Review Questions

CHAPTER TWELVE—CAUSALITY IN MATERIAL BEINGS

191

INDEX OF NAMES

No references are made to the summaries. The arabic numerals refer to the marginal numbers of the text.

INDEX OF SUBJECT MATTER

No reference is made to the summaries. The numerals refer to the marginal numbers.

Abstraction, degrees of 22 ff.; absolute space and, 100; absolute time and, 112.

Accidents, substantial change and, 44; quantity as, 72; quality as, 136, 140, 142.

Act, motion as, 81 f. See *Form, Hylomorphism, Substance, Accident.*

Action, at a distance, 52, 64; of form, 51.

Aggregate, substance and, 56.

Alteration, 43 f., 81, 137 ff.

Analogy, of metaphysical principles, 11; of essence, 28; of hylomorphic composition, 31; of species, 28, 32; of substance, 32; of time with place (space), 109; of quantity, 134; of cause and effect, 146; of finality, 155.

Analysis, 10; of scientific propositions, 17; of scientific methods, 18; of motion, 81.

Atoms, permanence in compound, 55; individuality and, 58.

Being, intelligibility of, 10, 66; matter and form as principles of, 38 f., 42, 48; material, see *Matter, Body.*

Body, essential composition, see *Hylomorphism;* spatio-temporal character of, 35; substance-accident composition, 35; motion of, 81 ff.; place and, 92.; impenetrability of, 94; multilocation, 95; of more or less than three dimensions, 102 f.; active power and, 141 f. See also *Matter, Substance.*

Categories, phenomenological, 20.

Causality, efficient and motion, 86, 131; relativity and, 118, 146; principle of, 147; spontaneous disintegration and, 148 f.; ambiguity of term, 148; determinism and, 150 f. Final and motion, 85; principle of, 154 f.

Hylomorphism, starting point, 28 ff.; substantial change and, 29 ff.; multiplication of individuals in species, 32 ff.; temporality and, 35; science and, 52 ff.; critique by hylosystemism, 68; quantity-quality and, 136. See also *Form, Matter, Change.*

Hylosystemism, 67 ff.

Impenetrability, 94.

Impetus, 86, 131.

Indeterminism, 151 f.

Individuals(s), multiplication in same species, 8, 32 ff.; analogy of, 32; of material substance, 57 ff.

Induction, 9.

Inertia, law of, and motion, 86, 92, 131.

Intensity, 134 f., 137, 140.

Insights, scientists and, 123 ff.

Mass, matter and, 52, 77; energy and, 53.

Mathematics, 22; motion and, 93; compenetration and, 94; space and, 102 f.; space-time, 114 ff.; qualities and, 135.

Matter, prime, 28; unity of, 34; reality of, 38; corruption and, 39; knowability of, 39; union of form, 48; nucleus and, 54. *Secondary,* 39; creation and annihilation of, 6; discontinuity of, 52; mass and, 52, 77; energy and, 53; unity of, 54; particles of, and substance, 58; not purely active, 63; extension and, 77. See also *Dynamism, Hylomorphism, Hylosystemism, Mechanism.*

Measurement, of time, 108 ff.; of distance, 115, 125; qualities and, 131, 133 ff.

Mechanism, free will and, 6, 150; nature of matter, 65 f.

Metaphysics, 13; philosophy of nature and, 13, 22 ff.

Method, of philosophy of nature, 3 ff., 9 ff.; analysis of scientific, 18; phenomenological, 20.

Motion, continuum and, 76; analysis of, 81; reality of, 83; divisibility of, 83; Zeno and, 84; unity of, 85; place and, 92 f.; absolute, 92; time and, 110; relativity of, 121; qualities and, 131.

Multilocation, 95.

Multiplication, of individuals in species, 8, 32 ff.

Species, many individuals in same, 8, 32 ff. See also *Essence.*

Substance, analogy of, 32; disposition and, 43; action at a distance and, 64; quantity and, 72. See also *Individual, Body.*

Temporality, 35.

Time, 108 ff.; motion and, 110; measurement of, 110, 122; duration and, 111; reality of, 112 ff.; relativity theory and, 114 ff.; simultaneity, 123 f.

Ubication, 92.

Unity of hylomorphic compound, 48; of motion, 85.

Universe, as one substance, 57; place of, 92; boundless but finite, 104; four-dimensional, 122; mechanical view of, 150 ff.

Verifiability, empirical, 3; non-empirical, 4; division of science and, relativity and, 123, 125.